About the Author

Abz Mukadam is a partially sighted entrepreneur.

Finding Salman is the author's first novel; he chose the comedy genre as he truly enjoys making people laugh. He is currently studying to achieve a bachelor's degree in business management via Open University, specialising in Innovation & Enterprise. He is also the founder of a few companies based in the UK. He has achieved all these quite extraordinary things because of his loss of vision. His life which has quite a chequered and colourful past has led to many unique experiences. He has a Peter Pan like personality where he is still young at heart. He has not allowed the harshness of his bitter experiences change him as a person and like a fine wine, his mindset has improved with age. He has a cheerful, optimistic and happy go lucky view of life and impacts everyone he meets in the most positive way.

Editors Notes

My name is Pravika Kapoor and I'm currently pursuing an English and Creative Writing degree from The University of British Columbia, Vancouver, BC, Canada. I discovered my love for reading and writing in middle school. I have been teaching Spanish to middle schoolers for more than 2 years now and am also a freelance writer, beta reader, editor and proofreader. I also own an Instagram page where I post recipes and book reviews. Feel free to connect with me on Instagram:pravikakapoor

Abz contacted me in March 2023 to edit his novel. It has been a great experience editing for him. He's been a wonderful and patient client. Even though we are in the different parts of the world, we made it work, despite the time difference.
When I read about his life story, I was amazed. He's an absolute inspiration. He's gone through so much but never gave up. Instead, he ended up writing a wonderful book on an important issue. He is an inspiration and I hope a lot of people get inspired by him, because I sure am inspired. Despite going through so much, he's still such a happy person and tries to make others laugh. I pray to god that I can always be like him in my tough times.

It has been an absolute pleasure knowing this man and working with him. I look forward to be working on his future projects with.

PROVERB;
> a short, well-known pithy saying, stating a general truth or piece of advice.

FINDING SALMAN KHAN…

By Mr Abz

This book is dedicated to all of those people who stood by me in my darkest of times. I did not have the heart to let you down, after you told me you believed in me.

Contents

Gratitude.

Personal Challenges.

No Offence.

Meet the Characters

Kindred Spirits

The Shakespeare's
Uncle Joey
Callum Shakespeare (Cal)
Samantha Shakespeare (Sam)
Harry Shakespeare
Taylor Shakespeare

The Khan's
Moskat Khan (Mozzy)
Maria Khan
Samia Khan
Sonam Khan
Uncle Raja Walid Khan (Zindabad)
Aunty Shaynaz Khan

The Maier's
Olivia Maier (Mamica)
Amelia Maier
Eva Maier

The Imam
Imam Hakim Malaika (Aka: Zesty Bhai)

Chapters

(Chapter 1) Silent Night. (Pg. 69)
(Chapter 2) Shariah Law. (Pg. 95)
(Chapter 3) Fish & Guests Smell. (Pg. 109)
 (When they're three days old).
(Chapter 4) The Husband. (Pg.127)
 (Is always the last to know!)
(Chapter 5) Blame the tool. (Pg.138)
(Chapter 6) Jolly Good to BollyWood. (Pg.147)
(Chapter 7) Good things happen to good people.
 (Pg. 200)
(Chapter 8) Marriages are made in heaven. (Pg.207)
(Chapter 9) Ever After. (Pg.217)

Epilogue.

Acknowledgements.

Synopsis.

Gratitude

I am…

Forever grateful, appreciative and thankful to my true Creator, for all you are doing, have already done and all you are about to do for me. Thank you for allowing me to have a tiny insight into understanding and accepting the in-explainable miracle of my beating heart. I feel it's movement 24/7 with praise and gratitude; It is governed by no one but you.

The Creator, who not only dedicated nine months to create me and give me the opportunity to exist, but he also never left my side, even in my weaker moments. He never let me endure a single day of involuntary hunger. He's the one who allowed me to lead an exciting, eventful life, full of extreme highs, unique, unpredictable and peculiar lows. He gave me the courage and power of an uncaged Tiger, guided me through anything I thought I could not handle or thought was above my station and gifted me the most amazing sense of humour. Dear God, I thank you from every fibre of my body, soul and being, for all the experiences, for giving me the gift of life and a big thank you for teaching me to forgive anyone and everyone and to have faith and trust in you, knowing you will get the job done.

I would like to take this opportunity to thank my loving, patient and devoted wife and my handsome, smart, hilarious, creative, and pure hearted son (the reason I get up every day). You have put up with me during the creation of this book. I could never have done it without you; from tolerating my mood swings and emotions, day after day, night after night, to having patience, support, and unwavering enthusiasm. I feel blessed each day to have such a fantastic team around me. I have often thought of putting pen to paper, yet never had the courage until some life changing events occurred. It made me appreciate that I am still able to read and write and to see half of everything in this amazing place we call Earth especially still being able to see my family smiling (yet occasionally disapproving) faces. I'm so sorry you are not here to see it Dad you would have been so proud. However, I do know you are always watching over all of us. I miss you dearly. Thank you for always believing in me even when I messed up.

I pray for you each and every day. I am grateful to all of the renegades, those who had forsaken me and left me to rot and die, your decision to do so allowed me solitude, whence my tale took root. It also taught me how powerful and valorous I really am, so a big thank you, to you all.

Personal Challenges.

A bit about some of the physical challenges that I have had to endure and overcome:

2013- I survived a Heart Attack, and was on the doorstep of death, only to be resurrected via my brother's CPR skills (Thanks Bro!) and a defibrillator en-route to hospital from a very capable ambulance staff (The Resurrection). It made me immensely appreciative and grateful for my very existence.
2016- I survived a Stroke (A stroke of bad luck? I hear you say). On the contrary, it allowed me to reflect on my actions and the implications that my actions have had on others. As a result of my stroke, I lost my sight and became labelled as Blind/Partially sighted. After this I was not allowed to drive again, however, I can assure you that being chauffeur driven is not too shabby. This also forced me to use the public transport system, where I met the most fascinating people. I also have a vibrant and tumultuous affair with Uber, Bolt and Ola. It also made me focus on how much I could still achieve. The best bit is, my son holds my arm as a guide (my guardian angel) all the time when we venture out, so I don't bump into people or things (especially those concrete stumps on the pavements. Ouch!) and then mistakenly be accused of taking drugs or

being drunk. (hooray) Sometimes you must go blind to be able to see.

2019- I was diagnosed with Diabetes one day before Christmas eve. (Being too sweet to everyone, if you ask me!) It forced me into eating more vegetables and going for lovely long walks, and also attending the gym regularly (ahem). All this Saturn and Plutonian energy gave me a new lease of life. I am telling you the things that I could have used or said to make excuses, to not even get up in the morning or achieve anything whatsoever. Instead, telling you about myself in this very personal way, hopefully inspires or creates a spark in at least one of you, proving that you can achieve and do anything if you really want to, especially when you are going through challenging times. Never give up and be your own biggest supporter and motivator. No matter what happens, know that the creator loves you and is always with you, ready to help, guide, protect and support you. All you have to do is ask him. Trust me on this, it doesn't matter if you have never done a religious act of worship in your life. He is waiting for you to ask. So go do it! If all of these things and much more, did not happen to me, this book would not exist today. Above all else always keep your sense of humour. One Love

No Offence.

All of the characters and the story-line is completely 100% fictitious, (The whole concept is purely a figment of my somewhat bizarre and slightly unusual imagination). The characters and events portrayed in this book bear no resemblance to anybody alive or dead or any tale I have ever heard before (However, I do believe a tale lies within each one of us). The story-line is not related to any actual events that have ever taken place. If anything resembles even a tiny iota or has similarities within the confines of this particular tale of something you may have heard, experienced or even seen in a film or read in a book, rest assured it really is purely just coincidental. This book was written purely in the name of comedy to instill a tiny bit of light, where there is nothing but darkness and is not intended or meant to cause any type of harm, injury, disrespect or offence. However, life teaches us that it is impossible to please everyone all of the time. (Please refer to the creator of all living things past, present or future for details.)

So please smile.

Yes, YOU!

FINDING
SALMAN
KHAN

By Mr Abz

- Meet the characters -

-Kindred Spirits-

Callum Shakespeare (CAL)

Callum took on his mother's surname. He used to be called Callum Brown, however, due to his father's absence he changed it by deed poll to *'Shakespeare'* so he would feel closer to his Uncle Joey. He had just turned 49 years old He was a smoker, a heavy drinker and a sturdy 5'8. He was as bald as a cue ball and had covered his arms with tattoos of the Union Jack to show how British he was. He was an obese man who weighed 120kg (about 264.55 lb) and was proud of it. He suffers from uncontrollable flatulence (farting). He was sure that he is happily married with his wife doting on him and making it very obvious she could do nothing without his manly presence. He is unfortunately, a categorically dodgy plumber. He remembered the very first time he met his stunning wife Sam. He got invited to a party and Sam did everything she could to get his attention. Eventually, she plucked up some courage and pretended to nudge into him whilst dancing with her friends. Him being a very handsome and a muscular chap at the time, caught her in his arms and that was the exact moment he fell in love. She was shy and could not even look into his eyes. That night, after he slow danced his way into her heart, they became intimate and he proposed to her that very night, but unfortunately, she had fallen asleep. So, he proposed again the next morning, followed swiftly by going to her parents' home to ask for her hand in marriage; it was like a fairy-tale. Magic, absolute magic, he told himself quite often. He also justifies paying hardly any tax as he does not support Sharia Law (he was convinced by his Uncle Joey, that this is where all the taxpayers money ends up). According to him he does everything properly by the book He was trained by British Gas (before we had to notify Sid about buying shares). A patriot, a true Englishman through and through. He hated what was happening to his beloved country, undercutting his prices, working seven days for peanuts. Bloody foreigners. He often dreamt about days gone by (Brexit is the ultimate revenge) when Great Britain was white, like sleet, purity and goodness covered over this beautiful land, an all bangers and mash, honest to God, true England, which had finished ravaging the entire planet and its inhabitants of her wealth, treasurers and military dominance.

According to Callum's version of events, he was once a promising football player but did not chase his dreams because he was busy (he did not make the grade as he was actually quite terrible). He was an avid fan of the now unfortunately Shariah owned Manchester City football club; those Muzzys had their hands on everything like cancer.

His father abandoned him & his mother Diana, for let's just say a "Lady of Colour" when he was 11 years old. His mother, depressed, bitter and twisted, drank herself into an early grave by the time he turned 14. It was then that he realised he was alone in this cruel bitter world. He discovered he had an uncle, whom he met at his mum's funeral. He was then brought up by his Uncle Joey, his mum's brother, who took him in and treated him like his very own son. Luckily, there was only a 15-year age difference between them and like Callum, he was all alone in the world too. It was his duty to educate him into how this country, this great nation of ours, had gone to the dogs and how it was their patriotic duty to protect and defend England. Callum had saved his hard-earned money to emigrate to Australia as this was where he felt his kind of people lived. He saw lovely beaches and lots of Caucasian people becoming pink like lobsters, drinking lots of lager and having lots of piggy BBQs. This was the life he wanted. He used to watch, 'Wanted Down Under' quite religiously which actually inspired his fantasy of migration to Australia. The kids were grown up now. Admittedly, he wanted to emigrate before his sons told everyone that they were queers/poofters/fags or whatever they called it nowadays, he would never be able to live with the shame. What did he ever do wrong? It's not like he was a despicable loser of a man like his pathetic father! Callum Shakespeare had stayed with his family through thick and thin, he did not walk out and leave everyone to fend for themselves. Callum often visualised standing at the edge of England and waiving of all the people of colour of his beautiful island as they left forever. However, his sons hardly spoke to him. It was all her fault, she mollycoddled them since birth. At least Uncle Joey was always there for him, as he was for him in return. Now he was a man's man, staunch, one of the lads and a true walking, living legend. He taught him about the evils of the Shariah religion, how they (the Muzzy's) are trying to slowly but surely steal Britain and hold it as a ransom. As a patriot he would reclaim Britain; it was his honorary right as an Englishman. He did not quite understand how this evil had spread in our land right under our noses. Thankfully, under the guidance of his wonderful ncle he would never lose his path. No surrender all the way.

Samantha Shakespeare (SAM)

Sam is a 39-year-old very vain lady. All she ever wanted was a life of luxury and to travel all around the world In her mind visiting the most beautiful and exotic places, trying different food, and to be lavished with expensive gifts and lots of male attention wasn't much to ask for. She was a hairdresser by trade, well a mobile one. She had all the necessary qualifications and did her fair share of sweeping and making teas for moaning old crones, as she could not afford a posh home yet. Sam Shakespeare was always called to the homes of the very affluent. She often thought of all her clients as her friends, even though the truth was that she was just their hired help. She saw how they lived their fantastic lives, their holiday pictures, their fabulous clothes, beautiful homes, estates, mansions, their wild stories of all the different parties they attended and all the celebrities and affluent people that they had met. This was not how her life was supposed to turn out. She wanted it, she wanted it all. Instead, she was stuck with this farting, tight fisted, short arse, fat excuse of a man. She could not wait to leave him. The only reason she stuck around was because of her boys.

She could still turn heads as all the gym sessions and beauty care had kept her in good shape. Her not drinking sugary drinks and not smoking but drinking plenty of water regime kept her skin looking quite supple and young. She always got a lot of male attention and was sure she would meet a tall, dark and handsome fella who was ridiculously wealthy and had beautiful curly black hair with olive skin and dark intensive eyes.

They met at her best friend, Claire Anderton's engagement party. She often thought about Claire and what became of her. Last she heard, Claire had a hotel in Spain with her man. They lost touch and never saw each other again. She remembered a man picking her up as she was pretty drunk, and her high heels made her trip and the next thing she knew they shared a kiss. A one-night stand turned out to be the biggest mistake of her life Yes, you guessed it, she got pregnant that night and panicked which led to them getting married and the rest is history.

She was just biding her time to make her move since she had been saving all of her money. Luckily, Cal had a misogynistic attitude and thought Sam hardly made any money, and what little she did make, all of it went on her makeup products. He thought she did nothing, and her pathetic little business was just an excuse to gossip with her silly friends and get out of doing any cooking, laundry or housework.

'Well, it's time up for sunshine', she thought. 'I am finally going to do this. The divorce papers have been ready for a while now.'

She was always fantasising about her new glamorous life, all the places she would travel to in first class and all the fascinating people she would meet over freshly ground coffee (with oat milk). She wanted to be a regular and on first name terms at the ever so glamorous and famous Annabel's in

Mayfair, London. The harsh truth was that she was panicking as she was not ready for the big 40.

I mean F. O. U. R. T.Y!

'Life begins at 40,' the older clientele had once told her

Yes, she thought you mean life at the doctor's surgery and hospital appointments begins at 40.

She had to move quickly to restart, it would be ridiculously easy, well, that's how it played out in her head anyway. She had her masterplan all laid out; she just needed a nudge to start implementing her excellently laid out plan. Every time she was about to do that thing (divorce him), she found an excuse not to do it. Blaming the kids and her friends.

Excuses, excuses, excuses.

The truth was she was scared She had never ever done anything for herself. Callum was a mountain of support and no matter how much of a plonker he was he did give her stability and a safe place she called home. However, her burning desire for a better life outweighed anything she had in her current life, so she made herself detest him at every available opportunity to make it easy for when she did the deed. She almost did it a few years ago, but then the arter took her to Egypt, so she thought it was not quite the right time yet, or had she missed the boat, and it was already too late?

These niggling doubts often clouded her thoughts; she always rose above them, her delaying tactics worked yet had run their course. She knew it was time, time to wake up and smell the coffee.

LIFE BEGINS AT 40, and the big four zero was smashing her back door down. It was a burning desire within her, it could no longer be contained.

'She had given up the best part of her life but no more, the phoenix rises from the ashes or cloud of smoke on this occasion,' she thought.

Harry Shakespeare

Harry is 19 years old. He is a very quiet, rare, gentle and a respectable young man. He looks like a handsome portrait of a Leonardo Da Vinci style white haloed Jesus with sparkling blue eyes. Some people say he inherited his mother's genes. He is a sturdy 6ft with an athletic build. He does not drink, smoke weed or shave, however, his beard always looks perfect. Harry had just passed his driving test and bought himself a very slick supercool black Vauxhall Corsa, and all the girls vied for his attention. He was not like everyone else, not after he had met Samia. His father wanted him to become a footballer, and, in all honesty, he was marvellous. However, his father would have had him carted off to the football trials and that would have been the end of Samia and Harry. She had changed his world. He was totally henpecked. Everything he did, every decision and move he made was based on him spending the rest of his life with Samia.

He was deeply in love with Samia, but he knew she would never go against her family. He had hoped that working at the shop would make her dad and mum like him and see how much of a nice, suitable chap he was for their daughter.

Harry wanted to marry Samia Khan, she was the most beautiful girl he had ever seen. He met her when they were in school and fell in love with her the first time he saw her. He had tried everything he could to spend time with her and to get to know her, but he told himself that it wasn't the right thing to do. He didn't want to hurt his parents. She was his best friend and he was her helper in all her latest voluntary tasks to make mankind better. Everyone was always asking him what he wanted to be when he grew older.

"To be married to Samia Khan," he always replied. His Pakistani friends told him the best way to get her to marry him was to complete five simple tasks, which consisted of the following:

1) Become a Muslim.
2) Volunteer at the mosque regularly, so everyone talks about you in a positive light.
3) Learn Urdu
4) Brown nose and suck up to the parents.
5)) Get circumcised (becoming halal)

Salaam Alay Kum (Peace be upon you).
Waley Kum A salaam (May peace be upon you too)
Yeh Achee Baat Hai (This saying is very good)
Yeh Achee Baat Hai (This saying is very good)
Taazah Halal Choozah (Fresh Halal Baby Chicken)
Taazah Halal Choozah (Fresh Halal Baby Chicken)
Muth Maaro Behno! (His friends taught him this, they said it meant let's eat together, brethren)

He did try and find a translation of it, for authenticity, but nothing came up on the searches. So, he thought it must be quite an authentic saying.

Unfortunately, it actually translated to;

"Let us Masturbate, Sisters."
Harry genuinely thought it meant "Let's eat together", and he often practiced saying it when he went for a meal with his friends. He would say it quite loudly and all of his friends would smile, and fist bump him.

Muth Maaro Behno! (Let's Eat together, brothers)
Ji Haan (Oh yes) Ji Haan (Oh yes)
Muth Maaro, Behno! (Let's eat together)
Meh tumsey pyaar karta hoon (I love you)
Meh tumsey pyaar karta hoon (I love you)
Mera Nam heh Hamzah (My name is Hamzah). This was his self-chosen Islamic name.
Mey tumahreyy bey tee seh shadi karna chaahtah hoon"
(I want to marry your daughter)

He was going to master Urdu no matter what. He practiced talking in Urdu in front of the mirror every day. He made a hand gesture similar to the Black Lives Matter salutation, whilst practicing and perfecting his language skills.

He watched Bollywood movies with subtitles. His favourite movie was *'Maine Pyaar Kiya'*. A golden oldie (super relevant to his life). It was a film based on forbidden yet destined true love. When it strikes, the lengths people would go to and the sacrifices they would endure to remain together regardless of the circumstances was somewhat overwhelming. He had watched the film over hundred times and was convinced love wins in the end and it can beat any adversity.

His Dad and his uncle were both on the same side and it would ruin everything if they ever found out. He could not understand how he would be able to tell his family the truth. His dad thought he was gay and his mum tried hard to get him to talk about his personal life, so he used to just talk about computer games to her. Not that he knew much about gaming, he only knew what he heard other people say. It was not a lie, just a deflection to bore the life out of her so she would stop asking questions. He worked part time at Samia's father's shop to make her mom and dad get to like him, and of course to see her every day. He had started reading the holy Quran in private, as he didn't want anybody to know. Being a Muslim would go down like a ton of bricks. He dared not to even tell Taylor yet, as he was not close to him, and he felt like he would betray him for sure. He had never been this brave before He knew some things were worth fighting for. This was about fighting for his love, his life, his Samia. She was the most beautiful woman in the world, no doubt, her heart was full of beauty and purity. She did not possess even a cruel thought within her pure, giving mind. He was naturally very concerned about what his friends termed becoming halal (circumcision) was, yet the sacrifice, he convinced himself would be worth it. He would build up the courage soon and tell his family, just not right now.

Harry was always deep in thought, preparing himself, playing out the coming events, as though he was David about to fight the giant Goliath.

Taylor Shakespeare

"Chef Shakespeare, only you can cook for the King, he has specifically asked for your expertise, and your expertise alone," fantasized Taylor.

He often thought he was born to the wrong family and thought his mum may have had an affair, so he frequently daydreamed of having a very eccentric chef as a father in some distant land. He was determined to become a Chef, a Michelin style chef to be accurate. Taylor was 20 years old and wanted to make everyone happy through glorious food. He is 5"10 with a slim build and brown hair with hazel eyes and looks like a young version of Michael J Fox. Chef Taylor's hero, idol and muse was of course the very famous chef, Anstey Harlot. Taylor literally admired this man for the heights of how far cooking had got the brilliant chef. He was completely obsessed and often fantasised of co-hosting a program with him. He wanted to name it Cook with Anstey and Taylor. He often tried to reach Anstey on twitter, though he did get the occasional like which made his day. Anstey Harrlot was Taylor's muse, he inspired him to become the best chef with the biggest personality. All he ever wanted to do was to make people happy. Anstey often came in Taylor's dreams and inspired him to become a better person, a better chef, to love and to be loved, always taking the higher ground and to put everything he had into his chosen art. Making a difference creating beautiful arty farty food, rejuvenating one's palate with panache style and grace. This is what a legend is. He was burning the midnight oil every night. He was not interested in anything else whatsoever. Man on a mission, however, he thought by making everyone happy and full, he could change the mindset of the world. After all food brings people together. Also people seem to be quite content and agreeable whilst eating in fabulous restaurants. He got top grades in nothing except home conomics. Now, don't get it twisted, he was not a born genius, he knew he wasn't naturally gifted intellectually. However, to get ahead, you must put in the time and effort. He was not afraid of hard work so this is all he did; no football, no friends, no nothing just cook, cook and cook. He worked full time from evening till midnight at a local Indian restaurant, as an assistant (dogs body/joey). He worked there until he graduated from the College of Food and Tourism. He was in awe of how the chefs received so many compliments, respect and a lot of requests to meet them and send gifts. He knew this was nothing but pure art. He even loved and cherished the process of cleaning up as it was all a part of the job. He was looking forward to his own restaurant; it would be a five-star restaurant.

Oh, how he would be respected and renowned throughout the world.

He knew that one day his art would reach the heights of fame because to his mastery. Taylor had a secret, he was driven to be so successful as he could not face the fact that he was not normal, he was not the average guy from Bradford. He could not even muster up the courage to admit it to himself. The truth was, he was gay. It really repulsed him. He hated himself and would feel sick every time he thought about it. To stop having these thoughts of self-discovery and experimenting with things that made him feel wretched, he busied himself with work. How could he share this with his mother, his father, his uncle or even his brother, a family who was lost, distantly and emotionally unavailable themselves? He just kept it to himself and buried it in his own heart where his secret was safe, and nobody could hurt him. Nobody but himself. He often thought if he did not focus on it too much it would go away. He did see a video on YouTube which stated that it was just a phase that younger people go through as they become aware of their feelings and body changes. How could a northern lad be one of those, sick perverts? When he was younger, he started cutting himself when he first started having these thoughts and became aware of his bizarre predicament. He knew his father would hate him and find him repulsive and probably never talk to him again. He stopped cutting himself when Anstey Harlot introduced him to the world of culinary art. This transformed his life and Chef Anstey Harlot became his idol, his muse and his reason for carrying on. He never self-harmed again, thanks to Anstey. In fact his influence gave him drive ambition and an optimistic outlook on life that no matter what, everything was going to be alright and to not worry about things that may never happen. He had accumulated a lot of skills and a very creative mind when it came to his culinary delights.

Uncle Joey

Uncle Joey Shakespeare was seen by the world as a bitter, cruel, deluded hardened alcoholic, and now a redundant Butcher. He wasn't always like this, he took in his nephew and brought him up as his own, showing him nothing but what he thought was kindness, fags, beer, bigoted guidance and compassion only reserved for white people. He never missed any one of his birthdays. He never let Callum feel alone or unwanted. There were deep rooted reasons for uncle Joey's bigotry he blamed the decline of the butchering industry, on all the bloody foreigners, and his traitor of a brother-in-law who also happened to be his best friend, who eloped with the love of Joey's life 'Marlina Karrot' he lost the two best friends, he had ever had in one go and the bloody 'Muslamics' for not eating pork, and shopping at the supermarket giants for their fancy halal meats. He was an out and out racist, so much so, he refused to even eat brown bread. He blamed them all the 'bloody foreigners' for ruining his life, and his beautiful country. He was a towering 6 3, a humongous mountain of pure unadulterated fat. should have been in the Guinness book of records with the amount of weight his knees carried every day.

He had long bedraggled hair, which was matted and looked like it desperately needed to be washed and cut. He was never without his long khaki parka coat and his Reebok trainers. Uncle Joey was a real, true, honest to God, pure Englishman, and was also a member of the honorary British National Party.

He loved drinking and having many meetings with his comrades on how to remove all the foreigners on a one-way flight to Rwanda, so they could return to their motherland.

When Uncle Joey was a young man, he was madly in love with Marlina Karrot, a vegetarian Hindu lady who originated from Punjab. Her heritage was from an ancient tribe of people who used to worship snakes. She was abused by her father at a young age which caused her to flee her home and into the arms of rogues. After many tumultuous and abusive relationships, she finally met Joey and they instantly felt an attraction. It was a modern-day love at first sight romance. She was gentle, kind, caring, always understanding and supportive in all his endeavors. Admittedly, she was obsessed with money and was ridiculously promiscuous. She was the original 'Tart with a Heart'. Her friends referred to her as quite hyper, nevertheless, they were to be married and spend an eternity together. Back then she used to massage his feet whilst he slept, style his hair and make him extravagant four course vegetarian meals. Joey used to call her daisy in secret. She smoked like a chimney and was quite ostentatious. Nobody used more hairspray than her, a fact she was proud of that her hair was always permed and she boasted the biggest shoulder pads in her little group of friends on nearly all her snazzy outfits. However, she made him want to become a better man.

In return, he was as happy as any man could be, totally content for the first time in his life, he couldn't wait to get up every morning at the crack of dawn since he knew a cooked veggie-based breakfast and a large hot mug of tea would be calling out his name.

So, what had he done wrong? He was left absolutely flummoxed, empty, numb and broken. His heart secretly yearned for her to come back. However the pain and betrayal completely possessed his being, each fibre in his body was filled with hatred and anger coated in an aching dull pain. Only alcohol dulled the pain a tiny bit. Well, it allowed him to sleep anyway. He put her betrayal down or rather his brain simplified it to an inherited cultural thing, as in brown culture, just an attitude of take, take, take.

The only way he could get revenge was to make sure nobody would have to go through the pain that he had endured, so he did something about it. By joining his comrades, his fellow patriots in removing this scum, these manipulative individuals. Those who came over here and took our British jobs, especially British Rail, the bus services, housing, our benefits and hijacked our beloved NHS. The cheeky beggars. He missed Marlina with all his heart, she was his past, present and future. She was the only person in the world who made him feel at peace, from within. He often dreamt of her coming back and asking for forgiveness and to start over.

The truth was his heart ached from the pain of her betrayal, it completely changed and broke him. He started drinking himself into a stupor, eating badly and smoking. He was a ticking time bomb just waiting to die. He knew his life would never be the same again.

His comrades often said to him, 'Never say Never!'

The hurt would never go as his love for her was expressed through all the pain he was feeling and he executed it as released hate and vengeance, but the truth was it was just a poison that he was drinking, thinking others were getting hurt, yet all he had done was hurt himself over and over again, feeling the wounds as though it had just happened as soon as he had sobered up which led him into a downward spiral of destruction.

Moskat Khan(Mozzy)

Mozzy had just turned 50 and was 5'7.5. He suffered from uncontrollable aerophagia (constant burping) which occurs more frequently when he is stressed out. He had lost almost all of his hair by the time he was 25. He weighed 97 kgs and was always clean shaven. He recently started to suffer from impotence and Maria, the kutti kept taunting him.

He was a local retailer who had to sell alcohol because of community demands. He felt he had no choice. His daughters were 20 (Samia) and 21 (Sonam) and he was slightly stressed as to how to go about getting them married off.

Mozzy was born and bred in Bradford a true Yorkshireman. He was an Indian Muslim, brought up in a Muslim household. (He is a Marathi, no not a Guajarati and No! He did not indulge in Karate although he did enjoy a latte). He was never really accepted in the Muslim (Pakistani) community as he was not a Pakistani. He was always introduced to others as an Indian, which would immediately get people of Pakistani origin riled. The only saving grace was the fact that e was a Sunni Muslim and therefore was not tortured all the time.

However, he was occasionally beaten up by Pakistani lads he had just met when they found out what his origin was.

The Indian (non-Muslim) people within the community called him a Sulla which is a derogatory term for a Muslim. He was a bit of a loner, so he styled himself as an Englishman with an Indian heritage, born and bred, he would boast. He was a foreigner in India (vilayati) and he was a foreigner in England too; he had heard the word 'PAKI' since the seventies.

Mozzy tried everything to show he loved his home, England. He tried his best to integrate and be as British as possible. He was an avid Man City fan; this was the only club that accepted him as a British citizen. He never had any problems related to racism in the terraces apart from opposing fans, obviously. He remembered the clash with Millwall F.C. in the previous years. It was a time of pure violence and the fact that Man City was Arab/Muslim owned made it multiculturally perfect. However, he was ridiculed, humiliated, bullied and experienced violent acts of racism by everyone since he was a child. He was attacked by Skinheads, APL, Mods, Rude boys, Punks, Glue Sniffers and Sikhs for being a Muslim and by Pakistanis for being an Indian. The right-wing organisations all attacked him and often threw bricks through his house windows. He opened the shop to claim his rightful place in the community. However, this worked out like a lead balloon as he was selling alcohol and was an Indian. Surprisingly though a lot of Muslims did buy alcohol on the down low for medicinal purposes.

Mozzy's mother died when he was just 12 and two years before her death, his dad went to India to get remarried and did not bother coming back as he realised that he loved being there. He did hear he had a sister from his dad's new bride, yet he had never seen a picture or knew anything about his new stepmom or his half-sister. His mother died of a diabetes related illness and Mozzy was never allowed to talk about his father. He was only allowed to listen to his mom thanking God that he was gone, and their life would be so much better now, it definitely wasn't. Growing up without a dad was the epitome of rejection and hopelessness, the admittance of nobody in the world caring about you apart from a woman you never saw as she was busy working all the time, trying to put food on the table for a wretched, ungrateful child, whose dad hated him and did not even want him.

Mozzy was brought up by his Uncle Raja Walid (Zindabad) after his mother's demise. He thought, as he was born and bred in England, he was British, a child of Great Britain. Well, to his dismay he was just a guest because of his skin colour, despite him trying to do everything to fit in. If you are poor, you are living off benefits, so you are a freeloading scrounger. If you are wealthy, you have cheated the system and stolen their jobs. If you have your own business, you are a Paki and have opened yourself up to ridicule humiliation and vandalism. He worked out that no matter what, he could never and would never fit in. He once thought about going to India but found out due to him being born in England, he was classified as a foreigner. He was a foreigner in the land he cherished and grew up in, in his so called homeland. He technically was an alien who belonged nowhere. He did not realise he was a bloody foreigner until he was 9 years old as every time, he left the house he would be attacked by the local obs yelling, "Get the Paki!"

It was quite acceptable by the local police who even joined in, occasionally, for fun. The local Asian community had enough. In order to protect themselves, they formed their own little gangs as the level of violence and hatred against the Asians was at a very high level. The truth was that it was just frustration as there were no jobs, no future prospects and everyone was skint. The comedians who dominated theatres at holiday destinations throughout the UK and the small screens

up and down the country took full advantage and based their whole act on hatred and disrespecting the Asian community, which made the locals acts of violence and racism acceptable in all the class levels.
The Panthers, The Bangladeshi Boot boys, The Redheads, The Godfathers, the list went on and on. It was a time of everyone looking after their own.
The issue was that he was not accepted by anyone of those gangs or communities. He chose to be alone albeit being attacked by different races, religions and gangs. He vowed to

serve the whole community in one way or another and decided he would place himself in a position of servitude by opening his very own family off license as he knew he would be serving all aspects of the community with cigarettes, sweets, alcohol, magazines and soft drinks. He thought he would live upstairs allowing himself to always be available to one and all alike.

Maria Khan

"I am just frickin' 39! It's not too late." Maria said into the mirror as she was putting her make-up on.

Maria had long wavy hair, creamy fair skin and kept her figure very slender. She was looking forward to her Salsa class. She was so impressed with how far she had come.

She had finally graduated with a first a 1:1 in complete secrecy. She had been doing a part time online accountancy degree for the last 6 years without telling a single soul. She also had a few side hustles, selling kitchenware and household cleaning equipment and Tupperware on Amazon, and was making a lot of money out of this. She had saved more than enough to start over. She had been taking Salsa classes for the last 3 years and she had gotten really good now.

Admittedly, she had developed feelings for her dance partner Christian, a Brazilian chap and she longed for his strong arms to hold her. That was her motivation to keep on attending his class. She always wondered if the feeling was mutual as he had many clients. Her Mantra was *'you only live once,'* that's it, you get one shot at life. Be careful how you spend your time. She had wasted almost 22 years with Caveman Bachan. She wanted to regain what she had left of her life. Her dreams of her future are alive again due to her taking the bull by the horns, taking control and not making any more excuses. She always kept God in her heart, but never really prayed, well, not physically, just in her heart. She was quite the entrepreneur and created a nice small business for herself. She had no need to keep stock or worry about fulfilment as Amazon took care of everything, she ran her little side business on her phone. She had a natural flair for business as she was quite organised and mainly sat in the shop allowing her ample time to: SELL! SELL! SELL!

And sell she did, with great results, her sales ran into thousands with a mirrored income to match. She was now educated and had wealth; nothing could stop her now. The only obstacle left was the removal of the wart, the inconvenience, the loser and the imbecile. She decided to implement the execution of her divorce before the new year.

How would her daughters take it? What sort of example will she be setting for them? What if her daughters turned against her? What if, what if, what if! What about uncle and aunty? How would she be able to face them all?

Snap out of it woman! She kept reminding herself on a daily basis. Those whispers will be the death of her. She had been thinking of these negative thoughts for quite a while and it was what prevented her from getting on with it. However, she was nearly 40, she needed to take her power back, reboot her life and live the best life for her as she felt she had enough with the sacrificing already.

Samia Khan

Islam is Samia's identity, she loved her beautiful religion. It brought her peace and tranquillity on this crazy place called Earth. She was modest, slender, had a beautiful voice and was breathtakingly beautiful. Samia had the most goofy sense of humour, this is what made her so unique. She could make people laugh. She always wore a different head covering to represent the different sisters and faiths from different countries from around the world. She was well known for doing a lot of voluntary work at the local Madrasa, harity shops and event organisations, raising money for local community centres, especially for the abandoned elderly Asian folks who were classed as a hindrance to the up-and-coming career driven Asians, who had no morals or values, just money and status. Firstly, they were ungrateful for all the sacrifices, showing zero acknowledgement their parents had made. They had forgotten their roots, religion and Allah swt himself. Some of these, what she thought were despicable people, did not even bother phoning their own elderly parents at all. They just sent some cash to them every now and then. She had a heart of gold and was completely selfless.

She wanted Allah swt to be pleased with her in whatever she did. She would take the abandoned, elderly on shopping sprees on the high street by pushing their wheelchairs or accompanying them in taxis. They all loved her; she was a saint and often prayed for everyone helping, assisting and providing support, without expecting anything in return. She even went to the local Sikh temple, the Gurdwara where she volunteered every Tuesday evening, serving langar to the people.

She was the favourite in her family, in the community and was so humble about it. Each and every situation in life is an opportunity to show kindness, humanity and most of all unity, this was her mantra. Samia was always sincere in all she did and was an absolute credit to her very odd family. Her mother kept trying to make her wear skirts and go out and do what she called normal stuff. However, she eventually sat her mother down and told her she loves Islam, and she was living her best life by serving God, the community and her family.

She often tried to dissuade her father and mother from their cruel, hurtful and toxic arguments. She didn't like that they were Muslims yet sold alcohol. She would often help in the shop but never handled alcohol or the selling of it. She maintained her prayers 5 times a day, actually looking forward to the prescribed time slots. She was not afraid of anything as she had God on her side, in her heart, soul and brain. She did not become holier than thou overnight, she was just born that way. The fact that she worked with all the different religious sects of the community had a lot of marriage proposals coming her way as many of the elders wanted such a sweet person as a daughter-in-law. She always responded with whatever God wills. She was the complete opposite of her sister, in fact, the complete opposite of her entire family, and often wondered why they were not religious. She tried her best to convince her father to change the

off license into a small community family grocers' shop or an Islamic shop.

"You must do what the community wants, supply and demand beta," was the usual answer from her dad.

Sonam Khan

Sonam Khan was an international star in the make (only in her head), she was a self-styled diva with Panache & chic. She used the best hair products, had fabulous skin with an array of coloured contact lenses, and had designer garments and nails to die for. She often fantasised of being with him soon, just to meet him once, face to face; he will be eating out of her hands upon their first meeting, it will make everything worth it. Most importantly she did not even have to change her name.

Sonam was very business oriented and always did everything solo as she found it impossible to delegate. She was busy 24/7 and loved every minute of it. She had a few employees; however, she never trusted them with anything of significance. It was usually the menial tasks, i.e., get my Mocha, pick up my laundry from the dry cleaner, etc. She had received marriage proposal after marriage proposal but always declined responding with,

"BUT YOU ARE NOT HIM!"

That usually ended any further conversation.
Sonam & Salman

Sonam created her imaginary world as though she was in a permanent 90's Bollywood drama (this included songs or background dramatic music to accompany events with fantastic sound effects), as she was Indian. She had never been there physically, however, sometimes she swore that things went into slow motion when something amazing was happening in her life. She was always the main character and all the people around her were her adoring fans. She had never left her home without looking like the celebrity that she was. She had a humongous following on Instagram. Always influencing, promoting, dining at the best places, shopping at the best stores, going to the clubs, pubs and bars. You name it and she was there, fabulous, Internet famous extraordinarily beautiful, sassy with attitude and balls of steel. She had a string of admirers, yet there was only one person she had eyes for and the whole world knew who her heart belonged to. She had a decent relationship with her mom who was always supportive of her. Her dad, the dinosaur barely spoke to her, he had this look of distaste whenever she was in his presence. She could feel the disappointment whenever she looked into his eyes, her dinosaur of a dad truly wanted her to become a doctor. In her opinion, she was kind of a doctor, well on social media anyway, octor of nfluence and photoshop. Yet, he was a typical Asian man, never happy unless you were showing complete submission.

She admired and respected Aunty Shaynaz as her go-getter attitude was infectious (even if she did have a very ancient and strange fashion sense). She was 100% sure of her success as she had manifested it her whole life and was still doing so through meditation and affirmations. She had a very good eye for fashion and being seen in all the right places. She had already travelled almost half of the world financed by her business credit card, which as far as she was concerned was merely a business expense.

She had a steady stream of about seven incomes on all her little side hustles which allowed her the freedom of living her dream lifestyle. The oddest thing she had to accept was for her to embrace her Indianness, as when she was at school, all her friends treated her a bit differently because they were all Pakistani, even though she was technically half Pakistani but she was also full Muslim.

So, instead of trying to blend in and become a sheep, she went in the other direction and became a leader in her own right, a bit like, Bradford's answer to the glamour of the Kardashian's. A lot of people saw her glamour as reachable and loved that they were influenced by her and her fantastic lifestyle. Unfortunately, she had no time for the degree to become a doctor her psycho dad had wished for her.

When she was a little girl, she told everyone she would marry Salman Khan and was laughed at, humiliated and ridiculed for it, however, she was one very determined girl even back then. Sonam kept all her promises, especially when they were in her little book of things to be achieved during her lifetime.

Thus far she had ticked off everything on her list, apart from two.

1. Get Rich ✓

2. Get famous ✓

3. Go to Bollywood. **X**

4. Marry Salman Khan **X**

Uncle Raja Walid Khan (Zindabad)

Raja Walid Khan is married to a Pakistani lady, Aunty Shaynaz.
His favourite words are *"It's my Haqq."*
Uncle Raja Walid tried everything to pass himself off as a Pakistani, so he was never seen without being traditionally dressed in Salwar Kameez and a topi with a bright and beautiful orange mehndi coloured beard (he resembled an ethnic version of Fagin from Oliver Twist), surma and a stick of Miswak (wooden toothbrush usually consisting of a twig) in the front pocket of his suit jacket. The tightest man in civilisation, he was so conjuse (tightfisted) that he would attend any and every function that provided free food to save on shopping. As a child he was given away to some distant family who had emigrated to England many years ago hey said he was a very clever child and wanted the best for him in a country full of opportunity. Truthfully, even as a child, he was very obnoxious and irritating, his parents couldn't wait to see the back of him. He was always out, in other people's houses, his car or at the mosque so he did not have to put the heating on. He would always cry the loudest when he went to console a deceased relative or a community member. However, this was to make everyone aware of his presence. He was a Taxi Driver (he drove a Toyota Avensis) out of choice, with a huge flag of Pakistan. He also had the British flag at the front of his house for all to see. In his car, he had a

standard I Pakistan dashboard flag and an air freshener. He was the very first, the trendsetting, original Asian man in Bradford who 40 years ago, drove up and down Wilmslow Rd, in a rented car, holding up the traffic whilst waiving a Pakistani flag on the day of Eid, and beeping his horn continuously without a care in the world. Raja Walid's favourite picture was above his fireplace, a portrait of the great legend, the founder, the gentleman whom he most admired in the world. He often talked to him, well his portrait anyway, the great Muhammed Ali Jinnah, especially on Christmas as it was Mr Jinnah's birthday.

He once could not afford to buy bananas, and this was his specific pinpointed reason to become the most tightfisted man to have ever existed. He did, however, speak only in the poshest Mirpuri language claiming he was a Graiyy (fellow villager).

However, everyone knew that he was of Indian origin which actually translated to,

DO NOT TRUST THIS GUY, HE IS AN INDIAN!

He discovered the late great Mr. Parvaiz Musharaf's twitter account and often tweeted to him, to accept him as a fellow citizen. He was the only person in history who was angry with his grandfather for not migrating to Pakistan during the partition.

Raja Walid's birthday was on the 1st of January, and he knew this would validate him for being a true Pakistani, as only authentic and genuine Pakistanis shared this birthday. He told this to everyone at every available opportunity as though it was a medal of honour.

One of his favourite stories that he told people when he first met them was an explanation of the origin of the motherland was; P was taken from the Punjab A from Attock (a district in Punjab Province of Pakistan) by Quetta (a city in Pakistan) and K from Karachi 3 pivotal corners and then the word ISTAN was added which translates to 'standing'. The majority of Muslims were in these 3 pivotal corners of Pakistan; hence, it was created with thought and intelligence.

Whenever he told this story, he increased the depth and volume of his voice, all whilst pointing to the sky with one finger as this gave him a dramatic presence. He was thinking of retiring in Pakistan, in his old age. However, trying to claim free land in Pakistan was a minefield, it was proving to be quite a challenge, especially as he was classed as an Indian.

As a young man Raja Walid, whilst growing up in England, he met and fell in love with a young lady called Meena who made him feel alive and wanted. She was his best friend and they were always making plans about where they would live and how many kids they would have and mostly how he would shower her with love and affection every single day. Raja Walid was also a first class cricketer. Meena would watch him practice everyday and attend each match with him, unfortunately her parents found out about this friendship, they were quite happy with him being of Indian origin, however it went against the NO BMW (Blacks,Whites,Muslims) rule and they then moved away to London never to be heard of again. To make ends meet Raja Walid would work part time in Axim's restaurant as a dogsbody. He was devastated when Meena left. A Pakistani chap called Talar bullied and beat up Walid everyday (because Raja Walid was an Indian) and had a real hatred for him because Talar's grandad, the honourable Choudry Abdul Majid died in the partition and Talar blamed all the Indians for it. What made it worse was Talar's dad owned the restaurant that Walid worked in. Talar set him up and got him the sack by leaving 100 empty opened cans of cat and dog food, saying Walid was putting them in curries. This changed him forever and his obsession to be accepted as a man of Pakistani origin went out of control. He married Shaynaz who was a Pakistani, however, she was brought up in a care home as her mother was beaten to death by her father, who was an alcoholic who drank himself to death. He married her so at least his children would be Pakistanis.

Unfortunately, the heartbroken couple were unable to have children. He needed Shaynaz, for she had a very positive impact in his life and had an immense amount of boundless energy. They were always supporting each other in all of their endeavours. He truly loved her and often said she was his heartbeat, and he could not live without her. Most importantly, she was a full-fledged Pakistani regardless of her family history. He often saw her looking at Pakistani orphans online and was secretly glad, as he knew deep down if she was to adopt orphans this was a step closer to him being a real Pakistani.

Aunty Shaynaz Khan

'The voice of reason' she called herself, and her husband referred to her as a firecracker. A Local reporter (who left no stone unturned, for the local Bradford Asian Radio channel), an amazing sense of humour, a humanist and a warrior for any cause related to females, a champion of equal rights, a lobbyist, for trying to make it a legal requirement for Men to complete half of the housework. Her husband was the opposite of her, yet they got on so well as they loved to debate about the current affairs of Pakistan. They often spoke of building wells around the globe. She was always frowned upon by the male dominated community, however, she knew the power lied in the women, it was just slightly challenging to get them to show unity and strength. However, lately the female community really had recognised the power of all the things Asian females could actually achieve.

She was a champion amongst the female community and knew almost everyone's issue. They all knew deep down if things went wrong, she would be standing next to them before they even mentioned anything. As a reporter it was her job to have her finger on the pulse within the community. Shaynaz was a master of outsmarting any man in anything tactical. A lot of ladies would send her gossip (sorry, I meant information) about every little thing, which meant that she was always up to date with everything that was happening in the community. Deep down she knew her husband was a good man, and she recognised all his faults. However, she would often overlook them thinking he will change as he ages.

Shaynaz was motivated by all the cruel rumours she often heard and saw how it destroyed lives, marriages and even led to suicides. She decided she wanted nothing but the truth. She even contemplated completing a law degree but recognised that a lot of solicitors lied for a living, again leading to scandals, suicides, bankruptcy, reputations ruined, etc. After praying and wishing she was around during the era of suffragettes, she found a release in media, especially, the local radio station as she was allowed a phone in talk show which addressed all types of women vs. men issues. The local MP (a highly respected and a very competent Ms. Maz Shahid) who had endured all types of abuse grew up with experiencing and witnessing hatred towards women directly and indirectly. Her mother was even arrested for making a stand and fighting back. She was her biggest supporter; they both often rallied a lot of support for vulnerable women. They had both been arrested on numerous occasions despite being on peaceful marches. They were quite a powerful and unstoppable force once they got behind something.

Sheynaz had often been to the Houses of Parliament with MP Shahid. To her, this was woman power at its purest form. She took numerous selfies with a lot of MP's to boost morale for the current government and to show how empowered the simple ladies in her hometown were. It showed that they had the ear of the government and the influence that they possessed. They had come a long way and the movement was very real.

Shaynaz and Walid had tried to conceive a child for many years, but Shaynaz slowly became heartbroken. She was like a mother hen in the community for all the ladies. She busied herself seven days a week. This prevented her thoughts from returning to the fact that she was childless. Her husband loved her, he never once mentioned getting married again. Lately, she has been seriously thinking of adopting or fostering children and was quite proactive, doing a huge amount of research on it. She had a complex over whether her husband would support her or not. She was aware of the orphans in Pakistan and the others around the world and she loved them all. She often visited all the care homes offering support, kindness and a friendly ear. She desperately needed a family, happiness, home, stability and security. Besides, it would make her feel whole. She felt everybody would embrace it as she had done so much for the community. The people within the community would be happy for her as she was happy for everyone else. She was very excited and thought how magical it would be if she was blessed with a readymade family. She knew her home had ample space and was already deciding colour schemes as she was not clear if it was a girl or a boy or both that she would be gifted with. However she knew with neutral colours she could hang up amazing pictures and homework projects, which she could display with pride. Shaynaz had never lost any battle she had participated in as she was always on the side of righteousness, she always turned to God for additional guidance.

She would inspire them to be leaders, examples of how people should conduct themselves. Shaynaz would fantasise at every available opportunity of her being called, Mum, Ma, Mother, Aamee. She decided to start the whole process in the new year and knew it was painstakingly a long process, but she had

faced many challenges in life and had not been beaten yet, her motto was " WAP " No, No not the meaning from the song. Smh. . . .
Just to clarify so you know, it's:
Women's Awesome Power! WAP!

Olivia (Mamica) Amelia & Eva

Mamica Olivia is a very proud and determined lady from Sibiu, Romania. She loved baking, it kept her feeling like she was achieving something each and every day, it kept her busy and allowed her to talk to herself when she was alone.

She had two beautiful, intelligent and feisty daughters, Amelia and Eva. They all lived together in Olivia's bed and breakfast which was run very efficiently, was always clean, had a homely, aromatic trace of fantastic baked stuff and bright beautiful flowers which she grew herself. They all lived happily in Romania at the time until the disaster struck and completely changed their lives. Olivia's husband Tata Florin (God rest his soul) and Olivia wanted to bring up their daughters with the best kind of education that they could possibly provide. So, they worked night and day on the picturesque little farm, cleaning houses, selling their harvests and washing clothes to help pay for and give them a very good education. Then when they least expected it, Florin met with an untimely tragic accident involving a tractor, a goat and a chemise entanglement. On his passing, he left behind a very small farm, a tractor, a distraught wife and two very educated daughters. Mamica fully understanding Romanian traditions and cultures started panicking and quickly got them both married off as soon as she possibly could to a couple of local farmer's sons One grew potatoes and cabbage, and the other grew Sugar beets. Unfortunately, due to Romanian traditions, the farmers wanted obedient, hard-working wives who did not answer back or dream of wearing foreign fashion and who would help them on their respective farms. What they actually got was two intellectual ladies with one wanting to become a computer programmer and the other a pharmacist, who were not quite partial to the physical demands of running a farm and making the food on time and to top it all off, they both had their own opinions. Within 12 months, they were both divorced, childless and dishonoured within the farming community.

So, the only route left was for Mamica to sell up. She packed her bags and headed to England with her daughters. Bearing in mind this was unheard of as no self-respecting Romanian would ever sell their family farm. However, deep down, Mamica Olivia was a rebel. She decided to lease a bed and breakfast with all her money and create a living from it. She grew her own vegetables, fruits and had a bountiful herb garden. She kept three goats, one male, two females, for fresh milk and cheese. She had a little makeshift well with live fish (Tilapia), and a few chickens for fresh eggs; their protector was a very proud cockerel.

Olivia missed farming so the bed and breakfast was the closest she could get to it. She really missed looking after her beloved Florin, so she named the Bed and Breakfast;

FLORINS HOTELUL CERESC
(Florins Heavenly Hotel)

Underneath the Welcome sign, it stated:

Să faci din, rahat bici

Which literally translates to: To make a whip out of Shit. This was Tata Florins' mantra. Olivia really missed Romania, however, due to the double divorce, she knew she could never go back. Amelia and Eva both currently work in a plastic factory on rotating shifts; they both continued their education through The Open university to graduate with a degree and fulfil their Tata's dream. They would be the first in their entire family ancestry to get a degree and become working professionals. They helped out Mamica whenever they could. They both felt compelled to be working professionals so their parents' hard work would not be wasted.

Imam Hakim Malaika (Zesty Bhai)

The respected and honourable Imam Zesty Bhai is a Ugandan born Muslim Imam and cleric. He is affectionately called Zesty bhai by everyone, due to him always carrying a bottle of bright blue, zesty sauce (yes you read that correctly. His favourite sauce is bright Blue!) He was always drowning it over almost everything he ate except of course anything sweet. A true angel on earth, a man of God through and through. He quite unusually sported a bright green turban so everyone knew the moment they met him that he was a pious and a devoted religious man. He spoke the Queen's English perfectly, as though he had been educated at Eton. Zesty bhai loved gaining knowledge. He had read his way through the entire Ugandan Lutalo Delta community Library by the time he was 12. Being an avid reader, he of course continued reading, especially all of the faith books which he could get his hands on, he found them captivating. This in turn gave him the opportunity to meet and bond with all the other religious leaders within the local community and around the world. It also inspired him to write quite a few faith based books for children; to teach them to be kind and compassionate, to have empathy and to be charitable and helpful. Apart from raising money for the needy he had zero interest in becoming wealthy or any desire for material gain, fast cars and grand homes. He was a doppelganger of the butler Geoffrey from The Fresh Prince of Bel Air and was often mistaken for him. He was regularly asked to sign autographs. He had set up a charity that would let poverty-stricken people of every race go on a holiday of a lifetime, it was an all-expenses paid trip to Mecca (The Hajj, the pilgrimage). The expenses were covered by whatever profits he earned from his little side business of selling Islamic jigsaw puzzles online, which led to receiving contributions from around the world. He decided to make it as fair as possible, so their local imam from whichever part of the world the person was based in, would have to submit a name via email from their community and they would then be randomly picked out by a prayer goer at his madrasa. He lodged in the local madrasa and was respected by everyone because he was of African origin and had many talents, especially other languages in which he prided himself on learning, he could speak Swahili, Latin, English, Punjabi, Arabic, and Urdu fluently. He is currently learning Romanian to help with the recent spike of immigrant prisoners, to get them through their hardships. He was unfortunately widowed, but luckily, he loved his job. God chose him to do this work and it filled him with joy in each and every moment. It gave him a reason to get up every morning as it kept him busy and stopped him from missing his beautiful wife too much. He was also the Imam for the local prison, HMP Leeds. The prisoners from every religion respected him. He showed them affection as though they were his own blood. He led the Friday prayers and then spent the rest of the afternoon seeing as many prisoners as possible to help and support them with any issues they had. If any prisoner's nearest and dearest were to leave them or leave mother earth, he would be on 24 hour callout and be the first point of contact. He was the greatest of empaths. He understood loss, loneliness, heartbreak and grief. He would sit for hours without even letting out a single yawn

and made people feel that he was on their side rooting for
them. He prayed with them regardless of what religion they
belonged to. This alone made him unique, a true man of God.
His humbleness was his trademark. He just could not
understand everyone's greed and obsessive hunger for wealth.
What was it all about? He always said a prayer for those
obsessed with money having no regard for anything else. It
was like having cancer, starting with just a tiny flicker of low
self-esteem and progressing into demonic and negative
actions. It usually stemmed from people who could not accept
why they were put on earth or why they were created, he
wished they would think like Socrates.

"He who is not content with what he has, would not be content with what he would like to have."

Socrates nailed it in one thought. Kindness and giving was a
gift people rarely indulged in, yet Zesty thrived on it.
Kindness was free as was good manners, yet many were quite
miserly, with something that could change a person's morning,
afternoon, night, day, weekend or even life and it was all free,
to both give and to receive. The governor of the prison HMP
Leeds, Ms. Dana Louis admired and respected his humility
and selfless attitude and she always made time for him,
always listening to his new and innovative ideas. He even
helped some of the prison officers when they were going
through difficult times. He was very slim and always carried a
positive aura. He looked about 39 years old, whereas, he was
actually 59. He was not blessed with any biological children,
however, he had adopted a little boy from the tender age of 6,

his name was *'Jamal'*. He had privileged him with the joys of fatherhood. He used to sit with him day after day, being his father, mother, friend, guide and study buddy. He worked out study schedules to ensure that he got excellent grades to get him into the best position he could. He was at university in his final year in America now, studying to become a Doctor. Zesty bhai deeply missed him, yet he held back as he did not want to hinder Jamal's progress. However, he must have done a good job bringing him up, as Jamal called him every few days. Jamal called him Poppi which used to make his heart cry out of joy. The community needed Zesty Bhai badly here, as he was always in demand, yet his mind often wandered to his homeland. He missed the simplicity of his old life, the fabulous weather, the smell of all the food, the unity and the fact that the whole community cared about one another side by side. He hadn't visited the place in a long time. His wife, had plans to go and build a little guesthouse to keep chickens and goats there and to grow their own fruits and vegetables, serving all-natural food with a huge smile, a clean room and an open heart. What a brilliant life it would have been. He kept a bottle of zesty sauce with him all the time as he remembered how he lovingly squeezed half of a fresh lemon with a sprinkle of crushed chilli flakes over his food before he used to eat his meals. This made him feel close to her again, as though she was with him. What was amazing about the sauce was that it was unusually blue which happened to be her favourite colour. Brother Raja often confided in him with all of his complexities, problems and his cursed Indian heritage. Zesty accepted him as a brother as he knew how corrupt, selfish and utterly confused brother Raja was e used to (he gave up after a while) patiently try to convince him to just accept how unique and amazing his heritage was, but it didn't make a difference. He saw him as a work in progress and decided that if he spent more time with him and kept him close, he would eventually become a better person. The truth was; Raja Walid, purely for his own selfish reasons, attached himself to Zesty bhai so the rest of the Pakistani community would accept him. However, Zesty was forever the optimist and believed that everybody was good and possessed compassion and love within them, it was just a matter of bringing it to the fore. Ultimately, he tried to do everything he could do; creating a platform to let people flourish in a nourishing, warm and caring environment, that would lead to a place of high vibration which would cause a chain reaction of prosperity. He was getting ready for the gathering at the Christmas tree with the whole community. He was just going over his speech that he promised he would say to the Lord Mayor, The honorary Lord Afzal and Father Martin who organised the whole event every year. He would be accompanied by brother Raja and promised to wear matching red Islamic scholar turbans, to show participation in the festivities.

-Chapter 1-

Silent Night

The Indian national anthem was playing on the radio in the background. The Barista was rearranging the Danish pastries and his son was with him, deciding which went where.

A very well dressed beautiful and pregnant woman walked into the Coffee Shop. She smiled and said hello to the young boy. She then looked at the handsome and smiling Barista and asked for a Mocha with a shot of gingerbread syrup.
"Do you want to hear a story, a tale from the not-so-distant past? " Said the beautiful lady.
She went and sat in her favourite spot, right by a replica of the Tardis.
She went on saying, A true tale which transformed a whole neighbourhood, in ways you would never imagine unless you understand the not-so-subtle transformative power of the lower heavenly planets
Uranus, Saturn and Pluto.
Do you know what the butterfly effect is?
She waited for a response from her captivated audience, they both shook their heads.

"A small or the slightest action can have a huge effect on the entire planet, changing many people's lives. You see, we are all one, we are all connected."

They both stared at her, motionless.

"Well it certainly changed my life in every possible way.

It all began on a magnificent star-filled night on Christmas eve in the magical or should I say Jadoo and Nazzar filled land called Bradford, where the water is pure, everyone knows each other's business, the grass is the most beautiful shade of green on the surrounding hills and Jinns roam the homes of all those who have heard of them or suffer from paranoia and mental health issues.

Where the locals live in a multicultural and enhanced Britain designed by the gluttonous for the ignorant. I share with you this tale as it is a tale worth telling," said Sonam, looking glamorous whilst sitting at her favourite seat at the Kokni Cafe, sipping her gingerbread flavoured Mocha.

Just then, two very short fat and sturdy bald men, one of them looked like a Pakistani and the other looked Polish, walked into the cafe with blue dyed flowing beards and long flowing Egyptian styled robes modified to look like the Man City kit. They smiled at her and went on to order two Cappuccinos and sat on the other side of the cafe, looking towards the entrance as if they were waiting for someone.

Sonam summoned over the Barista and his son. They sat down on the huge leather sofa next to her and started to listen to her intriguing story.

"Once upon a time, not so far away and not so long ago in the enchanted kingdom of Bradistan," said Sonam to set the scene.

"T'was' a cold and frosty Christmas eve,

England and her dog were getting ready for Christmas, preparing for a proper, bootiful traditional Christmas. The faint aroma of Spices, Tandoori Chicken, Cigarette smoke and fresh naans enveloped the evening air."

Fa la la la la, la la la la Fa la la la la, la la la la
Oh no no
Deck the halls with boughs of holly
Fa la la la la, la la la la (fa la la la la, la la la la)
'Tis the season to be jolly. Fa la la la la, la la la la (fa la la la la, la la la la)

(Adhan (Islamic call to prayer) was heard everywhere.)

Muslim worshippers gathered at the mosque preparing for prayer, the call for prayer was performed to alert all that it was time for prayer.

Allahu Akbar Allahu Akbar (God is the greatest)
Allahu Akbar Allahu Akbar (God is the greatest)

Meanwhile, at the extremely decorated and full on
 mas fairy light displays complete with a brightly lit Santa and sleigh on the roof of the Shakespeare's family home.The usual conversation of getting a drink before going out was just getting started Callum said, continuously farting loudly. "Darling,"

"Babe, I know, I know it's Christmas," said Callum. At the same time Sam was thinking,

When will it be the right moment to say she wants a divorce? She carried the papers everywhere with her; she just wanted it to be an exciting event as strange as that sounds, which is a lot more than her marriage had been, ready to be signed and dated. She reminisced about Eastenders when Dirty Den handed his wife Angie her divorce papers on Christmas day. How super awesome and apt that would be.

The only thing that worried her was how the boys would take it. She was 100% sure they would not even notice. All they were ever interested in was their computer games, smartphones and their textbooks. Their father didn't spend any time with them, and they are now adults. Old enough to vote, get married, leave home and pay their own way.

"Okay, fine!"

"It's Christmas eve can't we all go out instead?" Asked Sam, already knowing the answer.

"We are going through very difficult times, my love," Callum answered, continuously farting in short bursts.

"We need to save money!" He exclaimed.

Sam turned the other way in sheer disgust at the waft of his revolting flatulence, mimicking him and making a grimacing expression, whilst wobbling her head.

'God I can't wait to get out of this dead marriage and away from this buffoon!' She thought to herself.

She wanted some excitement, romance, wealth and glamour in her life but was gifted with farts instead.

At the local off license, which was called; 'Khans of Beer"

Pronounced, 'Cans of beer,' which Mozzy thought was genius, as he had thought of it.

"Happy Christmas Mr. Singh (Whilst releasing a silent yet preposterously releasing aroma from his rear end)," said Callum mischievously and muttering bloody curry munchers, under his breath at the same time.

"Hello sir, a very Happy Christmas to you and your family," said Mozzy whilst burping.

'Peyn Chodah, Ghundah Gora,' muttered Mozzy under his breath.

Callum, as a gesture of seasonal goodwill, farted twice.

"All Pakistanis love the English. If it wasn't for us English people, Pakistan would never have existed. You would all still be bloody Indians," said the arrogant plumber.

"Yes, I think you are quite correct, a lot of Pakistani men prefer sleeping with blondes. Maybe it's their way of saying, thank you for creating Pakistan. It's Christmas eve after all, just 12 cans Sir?" replied Mozzy with a hint of sarcasm.

Callum was gobsmacked and at a loss for words.

"Maybe a little whiskey too?" Asked Mozzy.

Callum not to be outdone, composed himself and replied,

"Yes, that is a good idea! A bottle of whiskey and some cigars, to celebrate this very English Festival."

"Yes sir, you are quite correct, Christmas is a very British celebration indeed. I'm sure Jesus was very happy here in Bradford, quite a hit in the textile industry so rumour has it. Furthermore, are you aware there is not a single white man mentioned anywhere in the bible?" Said Mozzy in a sarcastic tone.

Callum let one real stinker rip. He farted loudly and deliberately shut the door behind him as he walked out of the room.

'Revenge is mine,' he thought and cackled as he left.

Harry popped up from under the counter. Fully breathing in the terrible stench, he grimaced for a second then began to cough slightly retching and shivering at the same time.

"All done Mr. Khan," said Harry, holding back the tears.

"Oh god, has my dad been here?" Harry questioned.

"Yes!" Retorted Mozzy, while curling his lip in an angry fashion.

Harry was just about to drop a bombshell. He was going to ask for Samia's hand in marriage. He had mustered up as much courage as he could manage.

"Oh well, here goes," he thought to himself. He took a deep breath and gulped, then started sweating profusely. As he opened his mouth to speak, Samia's mum walked into the room.

"Oi Kutte! Close the shop now, all the other shops have closed! Come on, spend some time with your family! Everyone is meeting at the Christmas tree to sing carols." Bellowed Maria. She was so annoyed with her husband, all he cared about was his poxy shop.

"We are allowed to close the shop and have some family time. You are the boss, remember?" Mozzy righteously declared.

"Astaghfirullah we are Muslims! We do not celebrate Christmas!" Mozzy replies, burping simultaneously in 3 sporadic bursts.

"Haan ji, now it's halal to sell alcohol? Besharaam khusra!" Maria replied, sarcastically.

"This business is a necessity, as is my burping." Retorted Mozzy.

"Go and look after my family, you are a disgrace kafir."

'Hmm, maybe not the best of times,' thought Harry. 'Maybe I could try again later at the Christmas tree.'

Maria hated him with a vengeance; she had literally wasted a huge chunk of her life with this conjuce (tight-fisted) caveman. Why did her dad get her married to this Oaf? She often thought. I hope he drops dead Maria often hoped. She only agreed as she found out he was of Indian origin and thought he would not be backwards like the rest of the freshies. But, of course, he had to be that special one.

A group of carol singers followed Santa in an engine powered makeshift sleigh with what looked like frozen solid, shabby reindeers which looked as though they had seen better days, attached at a very uneven angle to the front of the sleigh. The Carol singers were singing jingle bells in a rather jovial manner with a huge procession of locals following.

This was the moment Mozzy was waiting for, rubbing his hands, he whispered; thank you god, thank you, thank you.

A long queue formed outside Mozzy's shop. He was serving customers like a man possessed.

Kerching! Kerching! Kerching!

He then went on to sell everything in the shop, except for the stuff his mate paddy brought in strictly for the travelling community. Only, it was illegal homemade potato skin brew. Paddy called it puchin, the brew was kept on the floor in plastic bottles hidden behind the counter. Serving the community, including travellers, was his mantra. Now, he could close the shop and go to the Christmas tree with his family. However, it was only to show that he was an upstanding community member and to show his British spirit (strictly not for any religious purposes).

Mozzy said, "The Khan's are going to the Christmas tree, to make our mark on our beloved community."
Uncle Raja explained he had to attend it to support Zesty Bhai and decided to wear a Santa coloured red Topi and Salwar Kameez to show solidarity.

"Let's go. We need to meet with the locals and celebrate together," said Cal.
He was slightly merry and wanted to ring out those bells tonight.

The Shakespeare's were all ready to go. With a slight slur, a drunken wobble and an ever so slight stumble, Callum stood up and said, "The Shakespeare's are rocking the world tonight "

Father John, the local priest had personally invited Imam Hakim (Zesty bhai) as well as the other priests from different faiths to the gathering; they often shared religious celebrations to show unity and strength in the community. It did bring everybody together, although it was often said that it was either the food or wine that had this effect.

'Silent night, Holy night,' was sung harmoniously and in perfect synchronisation by the carol singers under the huge beautifully decorated tree.

Samia handed out hot chocolate, gingerbread cookies (halal and handmade, of course) to everyone, with her willing volunteer and helper Harry.

The salvation army was out in full uniform singing in a perfected pitch.

> *Silent night, holy night!*
> *All is calm, all is bright.*
> *Round yon Virgin, Mother and Child.*
> *Holy infant so tender and mild,*
> *Sleep in heavenly peace,*
> *Sleep in heavenly peace.*

A Shooting star streamed across the beautiful sky which was adorned in all her glory by the beautiful full moon....
Followed by the whispers of one million wishes from all who were blessed to see her assail pass.
The whole community looked up in wonderment and held their breath as they looked up at the sky in awe.
Tiny flakes of snow started to delicately kiss and carefully snuggle all that it could land on ....

It was a perfect Christmas Eve

Samia with a very stern looking Harry in tow, carried plates of halal cookies, marshmallows and hot chocolate on a huge silver platter and offered them to all to enhance the festive cheer.

The locals lit up a multi-colored array of lanterns and sent them up into the beautiful night sky to remember those who had passed away. It was a beautiful and elegant gesture. The scenery looked magical, the tiny minute snowflakes and the dancing wind, a perfect combination that elevated the illuminated wonderful lanterns, filling the sky with a plethora of beautiful bright colours like an oriental festival which represented everyone of every colour throughout the world.

Zesty was getting quite emotional as he watched the lanterns float higher and higher. His heart ached to see his wife again, to experience her purity and her kindness. He missed her beautiful face and her loving smile. A stream of tears ran down his cheeks, onto his beard and formed a string of transparent pearls.

My lord, my creator, please tell her I miss her so, and I think about her every day. I promise if you permit, I will fulfil her dream before I join her.

"Come now dear brother, would you like to say a few words?" Asked Father Martin, interrupting Zesty's thoughts and prayers.

Zesty bhai composed himself and started walking slowly towards the huge, decorated tree. Behind him, Raja Walid walked with an air of arrogance and a most regal swagger, waiving royally at the crowd as he passed them. Zesty looked to the left and saw Rabbi Rudy, this now very old and distinguished gentleman looked back at him and smiled Zesty bhai reached out for his hand and then held it with love and admiration, gesturing for him to join him. They were old friends, Rabbi Rudy was very touched at the kindness of Zesty and opted to walk with him. Rudy reached out his other hand and formed a human chain with the honourable priest from the Shree Lakshmi Narayan Hindu temple. He in turn held out his hand to the Giani from the Guru Gobind Singh Gurdwara, who in turn held out his hand to the respected priest from the Kashyapa Buddhist Centre. A small stage had been set up for the sermon. What a divine gathering in the name of God and country. As the chain grew, it accidentally squeezed out Raja Walid, leaving him deflated and irrelevant. Upon reaching the stage, Zesty bhai cleared his throat.

"My dear Brothers and Sisters, we have all been brought together to celebrate our community. We stand together in all seasons, through good and bad times. As we age, we understand the importance of family ties and the power of being one. The strength in our community spirit has never wavered. I am so privileged and blessed to belong to a whole community who I see as my very own family, as we know family is everything."

"Muppet." Whispered uncle Joey.
"Why is he even here? Why has he got a rag on his head, turbanator? Is he a Blakistani?" Questioned Cal.

"Ssshhhhhushhhh!" Seethed Samantha.
"All of us on this planet, we call home, have one thing in common, one thing we all need to cherish and strive towards, whether we are born here or are migrants, if we work in banks or our beloved corner shops, if you are a humble street sweeper, plumber, tradesman or a businessman or businesswoman, priest, imam, nun or even an atheist, regardless of colour, creed or deluded superiority, we all need to be loved and to give love. We witness the effects of not being loved and how it ends every day on our screens. If you feel unloved, know that your lord from within the depths of your mothers womb, spent 9 months to make you in your perfect form, if you feel not cared for, take some time to show the kindness that you wished you would have had or even pass on the kindness you have received. As human beings from different backgrounds, it is surely our duty to love one another otherwise we can all say we failed at life.

"Here we go," whispered Joey. "It's collection time for the terrorists."

"So, I ask, if you all accept changes that are happening around us and focus on how we can help, assist and guide each other, we can all get to a better place together both here and the hereafter. We have all lit these beautiful lanterns together to remember our loved ones who have passed away, in unity and togetherness. Let us continue with these celebrations into the new year.

I have seen and witnessed as I am sure you all have,

If you want to celebrate charity, human existence, mankind, womanhood then go and spend a day with a Hindu family.

If you want to experience protection, and acts of charity go and spend a day with a Sikh family.

If you want to experience charity, helping each other and the inclusion of living things then spend a day with a Buddhist family.

If you want to experience compassion, forgiveness and acts of charity then spend a day with a Christian family.

If you want to experience charity, confession and seek forgiveness then spend a day with a Catholic family.

If you want to experience charity, devotion to god through prayer and fasting then spend a day with a Muslim family.

If you want to debate about existence and do charitable acts, then spend the day with an atheist.

If you want to see one of the old religions, charity and the devotion of a mother then stay with a Jewish family for a day.

May God bless you all." Everybody cheered and started singing. It was a beautiful and memorable night.

Everyone had finally come together as one.

"We wish you a Merry Christmas and a Happy New year," everyone cheered.

Father Martin had a few words to say but felt Imam Zesty had nailed it. Instead, he hugged Zesty Bhai and raised his voice.

"Jesus loves you all, please come to mass at midnight to join us and celebrate with prayer."
The carol singers burst into song with everyone else enjoying the entertainment and ambience, clapping and joining in with glee and good tidings for each other, including the patriots. A few youngsters chased each other with mistletoe on their hats, trying to get a kiss.

The soft wind carried the coloured seemingly magical lanterns on this beautiful, picturesque night, creating a merry dance, high up across the city. What a beautiful display it was. A few of the lanterns clustered together causing an angelic looking fusion; the cluster of lanterns sailed up across the peaceful sky unbeknownst to the rest of the merrymakers. Unfortunately the light breeze swept the cluster and got caught up into Raja Walid's pride and passion; huge Pakistani and British flagpoles wavering on the outside of his house. The flags entwined and unknown to all, would ignite a change in almost everyone's lives."

Sonam took a sip of her Mocha, enjoying the sweet flavour and continued in her tale. The Barista was hooked, caught up in the storyline. He had to hear it to the end, he no longer cared about the closing time and stopped clockwatching.

Sonam continued her story with enthusiasm and intes

" Then suddenly without warning, the cluster of lanterns, flew closer and closer to Raja Walids home until a gentle breeze blew them into the entwined flags and became entangled with the flags, which in turn caused them to combust and break out into fierce flames which then reached the flagpoles fuelling the fire. The intense heat caused the window frames to start melting. Within seconds the top of the house was an inferno. Simultaneously at Callum's house, a tiny leak from his fancy pipework (which he plumbed a month ago) within the stud wall of his bedroom, suddenly let loose. Gallons of water squirted out at a ferocious rate, filling the entire house with water. The pipe then completely exploded due to the pressure and within minutes flooded the entire house, it then started to gush out onto the road. Meanwhile, back at Mozzy's off licence, Mozzy had always used a long extension from one end of the shop to the other. Admittedly, it was very dated, with a lot of electrical tape in different parts along the cord; it was quite grubby and discoloured. A miniscule spark ignited the extension lead and immediately caused an electrical explosion causing everything to go up in flames, the very flammable carpet caught fire which spread very quickly due to the hidden 'Puchin' the wild and ruthless spread of the flames caused the gas bottles at the rear of the shop to explode and cause a thunderous noise.

Harry decided it's now or never, he had never ever been so brave in his entire life. This was his moment, the moment of truth, all that he had waited for. He took a sharp intake of breath and took Samia's hand. "Harry! What are you doing? Are you okay? I am a Muslim we don't hold the hands with men unless they are our husbands," screeched Samia.

He marched up to Taylor and his parents and asked them to come with him, as he wanted to announce something. Callum had dreaded this day for a while now, however, he was drunk and really wanted a bit of drama, so they all followed him towards the Khan's.

"Harry? What is wrong with you?" Shouted Samia.

Harry went down on one knee, facing the Khan and the Shakespeare clans.

"Mr. and Mrs. Khan, Mum and Dad, I have something to tell you all. Please hear me out first and then do and say as you please." Said Harry, assertively.
A multitude of thoughts went through everyone's minds.
'Oh my God! He is going to come out, right here, right now in front of everyone. I wish the ground would swallow me up. My son is gay. I'm ruined, and to top it all off, everyone I know is here. Why was Harry holding the Muslamic girl's hand?' Thought Callum.

'What in God's name is wrong with Harry? And why is he holding my wrist so aggressively,' Samia thought to herself.

'Why is this kaffir helper boy holding my daughter like this?' Thought Mozzy.

'OMG! I hope my mascara is not ruined.' Thought Sonam.

'What is going on here?' Thought Uncle Joey.

'What beautiful shoes,' thought Taylor whilst looking at Sonam's heels.

'I am going to tell him I want a divorce, now! It is the moment of truth.' Thought Sam.

'I have a strange suspicion about this. It does not look good and I will be stuck with the tightfisted floppy idiot for the rest of my life. I will leave him now, I am ready.' Thought Maria.

In a very strong northern english accent, Harry yelled, "LAH ILAH HAH ILLAL LAH HU MUHAMMED UR RASOOL ALLAH," at the top of his voice.

Now he had everyones attention.

"I identify as a Muslim now, a revert. I believe in no other god but the one god and Muhammed is the messenger of God" shouted Harry, literally translating his earlier arabic statement. I will now be known as 'Hamza Shakespeare'. I am very much in love with the pure, virtuous and beautiful, Samia Khan. From the very first time I laid my eyes on her, I was smitten. My soul belongs to her, and I exist solely to make her happy. I, with respect and honour, Hamza Shakespeare, seek permission and ask of you Mr. and Mrs. Khan for her hand in marriage. I have been saving up forever just so I can pay for our own wedding, so there will be no financial burden placed upon you. I ask in front of everyone to show nothing untoward has taken place and neither will it without your blessings. I am of those keen to maintain the Khan family's respect and honour to remain intact."

Harry had been rehearsing the speech in front of the mirror long enough for this moment. He just hoped that his pronunciation would be perfect.

He raised his arms to the entire congregation and raised his voice and shouted out:

"Let us all, Muth Maaro, Behno! As we are all one."
(Let us all Masturbate Sisters!)

The Muslim ladies in the crowd gasped simultaneously in utter disbelief at what they had just heard him say, covering their ears and saying,

"Tau-bah, Tau-bah"
(I repent, I repent)

Even his dodgy Urdu teaching friends were shaking their heads side to side, frantically trying to get him to shut up as they knew he would snitch on them saying they taught him to say that. It was just a bit of harmless fun, they had no idea it would be said in public in front of everyone, and as a speech to a very public marriage proposal. It was at this point they knew they had messed up and decided to try and make a sharp exit.

"Father, Mother I will now be known as Hamzah Shakespeare, I am now a Muslim and invite you all to embrace the one true religion so that you will be one of those who enter paradise." Said a very determined Hamzah.

"WHATTTT!" Almost everyone gasped at the same time, in shock and amazement.

'He is not a fag! What the hell? So, he is not a fag, but he is a Muzlamic? I don't know which is worse,' thought Callum.

"I don't bloody think so, I forbid this!" Stuttered Callum. He was geared up to have the talk about the birds and the bees and about Adam and eve, not Adam and Steve but never in his life did he think his own non gay son was converting into a Muslamic right under his nose.

His unembellished mind just did not know how to cope with Harry's announcement.

"Harry! You could have asked me first! " Said a gobsmacked and now very embarrassed Samia.
"You let them get to you," shouted Uncle Joey and shook his head in utter disbelief. Now he knew how real the threat of a Muslamic takeover in his beautiful Great Britain was.
"You disrespectful anima ou filthy beast! How dare you put your hand on my daughter! My answer is NO, NO AND NO! I will never allow my daughter to marry you!" Yelled Mozzy, hysterically.
 "Maybe, maybe if you can get Salman Khan to come to me personally and ask for my permission for this marriage to go ahead, I will agree. Now take your filthy white hand of my

daughter's. Furthermore, you are fired!" Screeched Mozzy ferociously, at the top of his voice whilst spitting saliva sporadically in all directions, in complete rage. As Mozzy was shouting, a shooting star flew up above in the night sky and seemed to burn out as soon as he finished. Samia was looking up to god and saw the shooting star. She wondered if it was true about making wishes.

"Congratulations you lovebirds, I give you full permission. Regardless of Salman Khan asking for your marriage to go ahead." Said Maria. All along she had suspected Harry's devotion to Samia was out of nothing but pure love.

"Me too, I think it's so sweet, good for you love." Said Harry's mother.

"Congratulations to you both, but who is Salman Khan? Is he like the pope?" Asked Sam.

"Not on my nelly!" Screamed Callum hysterically.

Sonam came close and winked at Samia and in a hushed voice said "You naughty minx, you dark horse, you." She starts filming on her mobile for her followers who lapped up everything she said.

"Guys an update on the wedding makeup, clothes, mehndi, hair and all types of beauty treatments. Make your skin glow baby! A special one for wedding venues, wow it will be awesome" said a very enthusiastic Sonam into her mobile phone on live stream.

Taylor was thinking of a 5-tier wedding cake and how many course meals he could make for the wedding guests. A little voice in his head kept reminding him of the budget.

"My beloved Salman Khan, you are needed. If you are watching this, please know that we need you. I will keep you guys updated. Stay tuned." Said Sonam to her viewers on her Instagram live.

Harry/Hamzah turned to Samia.

"Samia, will you marry me? I love you and always have. In sha allah I will devote my life to making you happy." Harry directly proposed to her.

Samia, for the first time in her life, was completely taken aback.

What had come over her best friend? At a loss for words, she turned to her father and saw his eyes filled with (50 years of being a victim to racism by Caucasian people) rage and hatred.

Samia blurted out "Harry!"

"It's Hamzah now, this is my name, this is how the world will address me." He replies, softly.

"Hamzah, this is a complete shock to all of us, can we discuss this later please?" Said Samia in a very dignified voice.

She then turned to her father and said, "Can we talk about this later? Let's enjoy this evening."

She went on further to say, "Papa, I will not and have never done anything to dishonour, disrespect, embarrass or hurt you or our family's reputation. I fear my lord and I am of those who are upright and pure hearted."

Mozzy stared into her big brown eyes and melted, then slowly smiled as his face filled with softness and nodded his head vigorously. She was and always would be his little baby.

"You and your sister will both go to India to get married. My decision is final!" Said Mozzy with an angry voice.

"Not on your nelly!" Said Maria. "Who do you think you are? Don't even go there. I also have an announcement,
"I WANT A DIVORCE!" Screamed Maria
After hearing this Sam knew this was the opportunity she had been looking for, and came forward, stared at Callum and screamed as loud as she could, "I have had enough of you; I have nothing in my heart except hate for you. I am sick to death of your farting ways, it's partly because of the farts that, I too WANT A DIVORCE!" Sam said in her most assertive tone.

Everything in Hamzah's world came to a sudden halt, Hamzah saw everything through his teary eyes in slow motion.
"What have I done?" He murmurs under his breath.
He was full of cavernous regret, he felt alone, empty and rejected. This was not how he had envisioned the fruits of his preplanned bravado. He had gone over it a thousand times in his head. A song played through Hamzah's ears, it was a sad heartbreaking song from an old Bollywood film. Everything seemed to go in to slow motion, the song playing through his head sounded out of sync and warped.
"Kahe Toh Se Sajna..."
Samia instantly felt very sorry for Hamza, she could feel and physically see his pain. She decided to act like nothing had happened and decided to discuss it with him and her family afterwards. Besides, it gave her time to process what had happened and allow her to make an informed decision. She did deep down admire how brave Harry was. He was always so quiet; he must have plucked up so much courage to make this announcement. Samia knew if he had asked her first, she

would have talked him out of it. She felt a strange pull in her heart as she recognised that he had taken the Shahada in front of both the families and anyone else who was present. He really declared his faith and love for her without any sort of care or reprisal. She looked up at the stars, therein she saw another shooting star, she took a deep sigh and under her breath said,

"Ya Allah, my lord, my creator, my everything, I will do as you will, I surrender to you my lord, everything you have planned for me, I fully accept and cherish. I am grateful and I really appreciate and am thankful of all you do."

Then from the depth of a holy night, the tranquillity and peace of what was supposed to be a perfect Christmas eve, a loud sound echoed throughout the entire area.

KABOOOOM!

A tremendous explosion deafened the night sky, destroying homes and vehicles, bits of debris, along with black smoke, flames caused havoc and chaos through the entire block.

The huge explosion was heard by everyone at the Christmas tree. The crowd screamed and started to run as panic engulfed all the revellers, running towards their respective homes, where the huge noise had come from. A mountain of flames could be seen. Suddenly, there were sirens, police cars, ambulances, anti-terror squads, the army and the helicopters surrounding the area. They immediately sealed it off. It was like Armageddon. There was mass hysteria, 6 streets wiped out in one night. Within minutes the services had arrived. The fire crews could not put out the blaze immediately. It was raging, they would be lucky if it took the rest of the night for them to get it all under control.

The local hotels were completely full, so nobody had anywhere to go. Father Martin told everyone to go to the church so at least everyone was warm and safe. The authorities could communicate with everyone at the same time and let everyone know when it was safe to go back.

Everyone was handed a cup of tea as they sat on the church benches. Some were weeping, some were silent, and some were in shock. Despite everything, the majority of the community was comforting each other.

The local paparazzi turned up and frantically tried to interview the locals and the services. Father Martin looked very stressed and worried, and called Zesty Bhai over.

"My dear brothers, our community is facing a calamity. I look around me and can see there is nowhere for anyone to sleep tonight. Do you have any suggestions?"

Imam Zesty immediately spoke, "Brother Martin, yes, of course. The whole masjid is covered in warm and clean carpets with showers and washing facilities. I think it's a better idea if everyone made their way to the Masjid and stayed the night. We have ample tea, coffee and biscuits for all. We also have new blankets that we give to the homeless. It would be the pleasure of the entire Muslim community to offer help, support and friendship."

"Brother Martin between us all, we can help the entire community. We are doing work for humanity, surely this is our calling. We must rise up to the challenge." Said

Father Martin, who by now had tears in his eyes. He was so humbled and showed gratitude to the almighty knowing full well he always provides.

The two priests of different faiths embraced each other with a deep gratitude for the unconditional support.
"Brother Zesty do not have any fear, we have ample provisions, and we can take them over to the mosque with relative ease."
"I do not fear, I know the lord is always with us and has brought us all together for a reason." Said Zesty.

- Chapter 2-

Sharia Law

An announcement was made over the PA system.

"Welcome to Al-Jamia Suffa-Tul-Islam Grand Mosque. Please feel free to make yourselves at home. Toilets are on the left and the main hall is straight ahead. Ladies, you have a separate section on the first floor all to yourselves. If you walk into the main hall, the volunteers are serving hot drinks, cold drinks and hot food with halal mince pies as a dessert. Please remove your shoes. Bags are provided so keep them in your given bag, so that they are with you at all times Brand new airline socks are also available."

We have made up some packs for everyone. There are additional blankets and pillows if needed. Also if you need any further assistance please ask the volunteers with hi-vis vests on.

Thank you.

The rest of the communities in and around the UK, saw everything come to life through the radio, social media platforms, internet and tv and felt the need to jump to assistance. All the other churches mosques, temples gurdwaras and other places of worship, local takeaways, local shopkeepers, all contributed and sent whatever they could including volunteers. The general public, having seen the terrible predicament on the news on Christmas eve, were ordering meals on social media and having it delivered to the mosque as an act of charity, kindness and goodwill to their fellow locals.

"Ladies and Gentlemen, we have made provisions over Al-Jamia Suffa-Tul-Islam Grand Mosque. Can everyone please make their way over to the mosque. The local authorities have announced that nobody is allowed to go back to the street as it is far too dangerous right now," said Father Martin to the crowd.

Zesty bhai reiterated, "Everyone please let us make our way to the madrasa, we have provisions for everyone."

"I am not a freaking MUSLAMIC! I am English. A pureblood, I am English. I am British. I do not follow Sharia Law," Shouted Uncle Joey. Some people cheered and started chanting, *'No Surrender', 'No Surrender', 'No Surrender'*

"Sir! Please!" Father Martin said. "This is not about your belief system, it's more about the welfare and the safety of our community, being together, and getting everyone to a safe warm place with food and hot water. Please sir, it's getting really cold, we must stay together. This way the authorities can update us all at the same time about what has happened here."

"Can everyone please make their way to Al-Jamia Suffa-Tul-Islam Grand Mosque, so we can brief you all there. Thank you all." said Chief Constable Raquel Hadcroft. Chief Constable Raquel Hadcroft was a straight up no nonsense, hardworking officer who worked her way up from the ranks in a record space of time through honesty, intelligence, hard work, tenacity and loving her job. She really loved helping the community, making a difference each and every day and she always went the extra mile. Not a single person had anything bad to say about her. Even the patriots thought she was firm but fair.

Chief Constable Hadcroft commanded respect and led by example, her kindness and sense of fairness was something her colleagues could not match. Yet, she could see through any BS from a mile away. She had earned her position through grit and always took ownership of whatever she had to deal with. She was not only a role model but a poster girl for the police force as she was beautifully stunning, radiant and emitted a warmth few could resist. She was a 7th Dan in Taekwondo and taught the youngsters at the local community centre.

Like a herd of cattle, everyone made their way to Madrasa. Upon entering, everyone was asked to remove their shoes. Uncle Joey and Callum refused to go inside, as they thought taking their shoes off was a sign of conversion and managed to get a few of their friends to wait outside with them.

"We shall never surrender! How can you expect me to go to the Mosque? This isn't Pakistan! This is just a ploy to make us become like them. I do not and will not adhere to any law but my beloved English Law." Shouted Uncle Joey.

"Just go inside, you lot! " Hissed Samantha.

"No way! I forbid you and the boys to go inside as well! We are not Halal!" Said Callum.

"Forbid? Forbid! My ass! Just come inside now!" Scorned Sam.

Right then the heavens let loose, and opened up, ignited by a massive lightning strike, and followed by deafening thunder. The rain poured down with a ferocity and force that caused it to rebound off the roads and pavements. The entire crowd was ushered into the large Mosque.

Callum and his fellow patriots were completely drenched, but were still holding vigil and not surrendering on the steps of the Madrasa. Samia came outside and gave all the patriots umbrellas displaying the Pakistani flag. As soon as she went inside, a fierce wind along with the now freezing rain created an unbearable environment for Uncle Joey and the rest of the mob.

"Let's go inside. At least we can keep an eye on their poisonous sermons." Suggests Uncle Joey.

"That's right, besides it's freezing now. My socks are drenched. I can barely feel my feet." Said Callum.

With a stiff upper lip, the patriots went inside. Samia immediately gave them a pack containing towels, blankets (that had the Pakistan flag on it) and socks. They were ushered to the shower rooms so they could freshen up.

One of the lads who happened to be a volunteer called Ayjaz Anwar saw the patriots and decided to be the joker of the pack and approached them with a straight face.

"Please sign the paper on the clipboard." Said Ayjaz Anwar to the Patriots. Callum was the first to sign it. As he signed it, he realised he was surrounded by a large gathering of Muslims.

"Do you realise what you have just signed?" Questioned the lad.

"It's for health and safety, I presume." Said Callum, matter of factly.

"No! Not at all. You have in fact given us all permission to use you to get circumcised!" He replied with a straight face.

Callum's face turned pale and his eyes widened.

All of the Muslim lads started laughing loudly.

"Assalamu Alaikum. Congratulations and welcome to Islam and the mass conversion centre, where your disbelief will be a thing of the past. Please walk this way to be circumcised, to the left is the grooming training room, and to the right is how to strap on explosives, second door to the left is how to steal British jobs, the third door on the left is how to get to the front of the council housing list and straight to the bottom of the corridor is how to claim benefits. You can revert to Islam at reception. Do not forget to leave a contribution on your way to the exit and we also have multi coloured lota's for sale to wash your bottom at your own leisure.

The patriots caught up with a horrified Callum and they all froze. It was all true and now there was proof of what they had done. They had betrayed their Glorious Britain by stepping into this devil's hole.

"I'm joking bro. I'm so sorry, I couldn't help it. Did ye think someone was trying to bum yeh?" Said Ayjaz Anwar as he roared with laughter along with the other teenage lads.

Just then Raja Walid walked towards the gathering to see what all the commotion was about.

"Brothers, please welcome our guests with the respect they deserve. It is our duty to make everyone feel comfortable and cared for." Walid said in a lowered tone.

"All of you, please make your way to the main hall, you must be so hungry." Said Walid as he beckoned the patriots towards the main hall.

"I've seen it all now, A Paki Santa!" Yelled Uncle Joey, who was still in shock.

"What did you just say?" Said Walid in a serious tone.

All the youths tensed up.

"You Heard Me!" Rasped Uncle Joey.

"Did you just refer to me as a Parkee? "Asked Raja Walid.

"Yeah, I did. What about it? The exact thing I said was a 'Paki Santa'." Replied Joey.

"So just to clarify, did you mean to refer to me as someone from Pakistani descent who happens to look like Father Christmas?" Questioned Walid.

"Yeah!" Said Joey, eyeballing Walid.

Raja Walid's eyes filled with tears. The Pakistan National anthem playing through his mind.

He was referred to as a Pakistani! A Pakistani, at last. Teary eyed and full of emotion he leaned into Uncle Joey and said,

"Thank you sir. I would give my life for Pakistan. I'm flattered." He said and hugged a shell-shocked uncle Joey three times from his left to right shoulder and then on the third hug refused to let go, embracing him with all the love he could muster. Uncle Joey, for the first time in his life was gobsmacked and at a loss for words.

Walid went over to each patriot and said, "Do I look like a Parki Suntaah to you all?"

They nodded and replied with a yes. Raja Walid beamed with pride. They went on further to say quack, quack under their breath. Mozzy kept running in and out of the mosque furiously, like there was no tomorrow as he had to keep on burping, and he didn't want to continue burping in the mosque and embarrass himself.

Raja Walid Khan was the luckiest man on earth. In the middle of such a calamity he was recognised as a fully-fledged Pakistani, he was so proud and so emotional. He felt he had fulfilled his destiny and wouldn't care if he died tonight. Especially as he had been recognised as a Pakistani by a white British man.

"Allahu Akbar," he said as he proceeded to embrace all the patriots showing gestures of his index finger up towards the ceiling and repeating *'Parkee Suntaah,'* smiling and wobbling his head with sheer happiness, as he embraced each patriot.

'What a madhouse.' Thought Callum but was suddenly curious about what food had been provided as the aroma reaching his nostrils was hitting him quite differently; it was making his mouth water. After getting clean socks and drying themselves vigorously, the patriots proceeded suspiciously to the main mosque hall.

Maria and Sam caught a glimpse of each other and gave each other a smile.

Hi, are you okay? I recognise you from the off licence." Said Sam.

"Oh, hi yeah. What a pulava." Replied Maria.

"Your Harry is a superstar at the shop, always helpful and kind. We treat him like family and the customers love him." Maria informs Sam.

"Yes, he is a good boy, it's nice to hear how well he is doing since he doesn't talk much." Replied Sam. They both looked at each other and nodded with mutual respect.

"I do hope they get married," said both the mums simultaneously, then proceeded to say jinx simultaneously and burst out into a manic laughter.

The delicious aroma of different foods from all around the world filled the air. The food being handed out contained steaming hot curries, freshly made naans, mixed grills, fried chicken, pizzas, rice, fries, Chinese food, plus some desserts. There were mountains of food and it still kept arriving. All the local takeaways, even the local halal KFC delivered food whole heartedly. They were heartbroken for the community.

The larger retailers sent milk, tea, coffee, bread, muffins, cakes and even Christmas crackers. The local Halal Butchers (Ibrahims) sent lots of halal turkeys to the local *Wingz 'N' Tingz* takeaway to coat and deep fry to send over to the mosque.

'I can honestly say I have never witnessed such kindness to strangers in my entire life.' Thought Callum.

"They really do go above and beyond, probably to lure people into this evil shariah cult." Said Uncle joey.

The patriots were seated in one corner of the main prayer hall on soft and warm prayer mats in a semicircle. The food was being served by the volunteers; it was an exotic plethora of steaming hot food from what seemed like every part of the world. Some of the youngsters found a Union Jack flag (from the queen's jubilee celebrations) and placed it before the patriots and served the food on it, much to the surprise of the patriots. As soon as they started eating, Samia came over and placed a new blanket over each of them, followed by a steaming hot cup of tea and custard cream biscuits. They retorted with a thank you grunt.

"I bet they planned all this, probably one of their suicide Ali Akbar bombers." Said Uncle joey.

"This time they blew up their own kind all in the name of Allah, no doubt." Callum joined in.

The rest of the patriots were secretly grateful for the kindness that they were receiving but dared not to say a single word.

This is Shaynaz Khan reporting live from the Grand Mosque, where an incident has occurred. The locals who are now technically homeless have found refuge in the Grand Mosque. We will be interviewing some of the locals. There has been an overwhelming amount of support from the whole of the UK, sending in food parcels, clothing and other necessities. I have been privileged enough to be here in the heart of it all.

"Hello Gentleman, Gentleman! Can we speak for a moment? I am from Bradford radio, can you please tell me your thoughts at this terrible time? What are you feeling right now?" Asked Shaynaz to the patriots whilst live streaming on her mobile.

"The problem with this country is, they are just letting anyone in, and this leads to these terrorist attacks!" Said uncle Joey with a very serious tone.

"This will keep on happening. They need to close the borders, shut and investigate all the mosques as soon as possible!" Said Callum.

"Are you aware that right now you are seeking refuge in a mosque and had they shut them all down sir, as per your opinion, you would have had nowhere to go?" Asked Shaynaz with a smile.

The patriot just grunted and looked away.

Sonam had a lot of makeup in her bag and was using her influence in the world of social media of which products to buy and wear in a mosque during a disaster.

"Ladies I'm here at the mosque and as ladies of style, fashion and just basically looking cool, we must always be prepared he world is watching us right now, so for a chic yet sombre and quite innocent look I'm using this mascara which as you can see accentuates a look of deep thought she pouted her lips as she talked into the camera.

"I have also got this headscarf which admittedly screams out, marry me and lavish me with gifts, so buy now while they are still in stock. Sonam said into her phone camera whilst experimenting with a multitude of different expressions and poses.

'Hmm, I think I need to plump up my lips. They are not pouty enough,' she thought.

Father Martin approached Imam Zesty, lowered his voice and said, "My brother Hakim, it is Christmas Eve. A lot of people are here. Is it possible to hold Christmas mass in this Madrasa? We can bring the Christmas tree from the church, the carol singers are on standby. No doubt everyone is seriously stressed and clearly suffering, I think a bit of happiness needs to be spread."

"What a fantastic idea Father Martin, you never cease to amaze me," said the Imam.

May God always bless you," said Zesty without a moment's hesitation.

He then began to explain about when the early Muslims had to flee their fierce enemies and sought refuge by the powerful African Christian King Negus.

He looked up and whispered, "thank you Allah."

As the Christmas mass got underway, a few of the patriots pulled out a couple of bottles and cans and were drinking outside of the Madrasa, much to the disgust and horror of the local Mosque goers.

They then progressed onto shouting profanities at other passers-by. There was even more uproar as the locals saw the Christmas tree being placed inside the madrasa. They were infuriated by the patriots urinating outside of the madrasa, the carol singing and the Christmas tree outside the mosque.

"Can't they do that outside?" They proclaimed.

Zesty conveyed the time of the Christian King Negus protecting the very first Muslims in the sanctuary, safety and protection in his kingdom. He also explained how nearly all the prisons in the UK offered the churches as a sanctuary for a safe place to pray as a community for the very important Friday prayers.

Nobody paid any heed.

They had missed the sermon on compassion and tolerance clearly.

"What an amazing sight!" Declared Aunty Shaynaz, into her phone's camera.

"Muslims holding the birthday of the Christ aka Isa al Islam at the Mosque, to show solidarity to the Christian community." Said Aunt Shaynaz as matter of factly into her phone screen.

Eventually, after all the authorities had done their investigations, everyone was allowed to go home, even though the smell of fire and smoke consumed the air.

Callum and Mozzy found out they were homeless and went into a state of shock. Uncle Joey had his tiny bedsit so he was okay. Aunty Shaynaz and Uncle Raja Walid had another house that had just been refurbished and was ready to be rented out hey even went as far as giving it to Shakespeare's Property, a local trustworthy etting gent who had a board outside saying *'To Let'*. It was just a small two-bedroom house, and the other room was offered to Maria, Sonam and Samya. Due to the circumstances of all that had occurred, it would simply be wrong to invite Mozzy as well.

Mozzy and Callum's homes, businesses and family had all disappeared overnight. They knew their lives had been changed forever.
Sam took her sons, jumped into a taxi and headed off to the local Travelodge.

Father Martin came over to Zesty Bhai, hugged him and said "How proud must your community be of you and your selfless hospitality and kindness. Be careful or they will start thinking that you are a saint."
Brother Zesty replied, "You my friend, are a saint, for trusting me with your flock."
Both of the respected men hugged each other.
"Brother, would you like me to stay here with you so you are not exhausted? I can take on the burden of helping you." Said the kind priest.
"Brother Martin, it's Christmas, go and spend it with your friends and family. I will be fine. I know you are a mere phone call away if it gets too much for me." Said Zesty softly.

Zesty bhai made sure Callum and Mozzy rested comfortably and had eaten well. He gave them thick sleeping bags, extra blankets, pillows and left them some toiletries for when they woke up. He did not disturb them or introduce himself. He did pray for them and was so grateful nobody had died or had been hurt, but mainly for giving him the opportunity to bring people of other faiths to witness the charity, kindness and the hospitality of Islam.

The three men who had not been the luckiest in their personal lives had no idea how much their lives would be transformed, all because of a shooting star perhaps. They were just about to embark on a journey they could never have planned for in a million years.

You see life happens while you are busy planning it.

- Chapter 3-

Fish and guests Smell
(When they're three days old).

The next morning, the smell of ashes still lingered with a grey cloud of sorrow over Bradford. The forensic people and the insurance people alongside the fire department and the terrorist squad with an independent crew from MI5 completed a full report. After much deliberation they called in a meeting with chief constable Hadcroft and said arrests need to be made as the public wanted answers.

The devastation was heartbreaking, it was grim and looked like Beirut. Moscat and Callum went there and were completely silenced. A whole lifetime gone, the ashes were blowing in the cold wind in a circular fashion. The two of them just stared and so many memories came flooding back of where it had all begun. They headed back to Madrasa, where god had them safe and secure.

Bradford was now the centre stage in the world of media.
"Was it a group of home-grown Muslim errorists?"
"Was it in the name of Allah?"
"Was it the right-wing extremists?"
"Was it in the name of preservation of the white race?"
"Is it a case of multiculturalism not working?"
Said the headlines through the News.

"Mr. Moscat Khan, Mr. Callum Shakespeare, you are under arrest for the act of terrorism last night on Jinnah Street." Said a very hard-faced chief constable.
Armed police surrounded the duo, they were told to lie on the ground and then they were both handcuffed.

Both of the suspects started a tirade of almost rhythmic farting and burping at very high volumes. Secretly, the armed police were glad they were wearing balaclavas that covered their faces entirely. They were then frog marched whilst remaining at gun point from several of the armed response units.

"One wrong move now and it is all over for you both," whispered the armed policeman. The confused and very afraid pair were frogmarched out of the Madrasa and into the line of riot vans and bomb squad vehicles escorted by police vehicles, motorbikes and unmarked police response unit vehicles, with sirens blazing and the blue and red lights flashing in all directions. All the news channels and paparazzi had gathered outside, zooming in their huge camera lenses onto the faces of the petrified pair with the whole community gathered outside. They just looked downwards as they heard all the swearing and shouting filled with hate and vengeance at them.

While they were in the custody, their wives went to the police station and handed the divorce papers to the custody sergeant. They did not even bother to go in and visit them.

After a massive interrogation which led to the obvious, that they were definitely not terrorists or part of any hate group. The whole incident was classed as an accident and the insurers were happy to pay out. The pair were released without charge, but unfortunately, through circumstances beyond their control, they were homeless. They headed to the nearest bed and breakfast, hoping to get a room and a washroom.

Meanwhile, the community elders had a meeting in private and one of them was elected to speak to Raja Walid.

"Brother Raja Walid we must talk with you in private," said the elders within the Pakistani community. This was the first time they had addressed him collectively; Walid was quite flattered and excited.

"Assalamualaikum my brothers, how can I be of service?" Asked Walid.

"It is a delicate matter that we need to speak to you about, our dear brother." Replied Zubair, one of the elders within the community.

"But first, how is your family?" He asked.

"My wife Shaynaz is very well, as am I." Replied Walid.

"May Allah always reward you both for all the work you do for the community." Said Zubair.

"Alhamdulillah," responded the gathering of gentlemen.

"Erm, getting straight to the point, not my beliefs or opinions, however, just conveying the message and often the messenger is blamed. The community's concerns are about Imam Zesty bhai, he has gone a bit crazy, and they feel he is suffering from emotional overboard, allowing the kaffirs, so sorry, I mean the non Muslims, to have a Christmas tree outside our place of worship. They are singing, *'Jesus is our Saviour'* in our masjid and everybody feels disrespected and violated. Yes, we must be hospitable due to the circumstances. The community is very upset at how the Imam has conducted the very respect and honour of our masjid. I personally have no problem, however, the community has spoken and furthermore requested that I speak with you as you are one of us, meaning a pillar in the community and you can relate to the Pakistani community as a whole. Therefore, we are requesting that you speak to Zesty Bhai and ask him to resign with immediate effect and in his place, we want to put a true Pakistani by name and spirit, that someone, of course, is you, Maarey Prah, Paiy Walid (My brother, Walid).

Raja Walid was shell shocked, his jaw dropped and he for once, was at a loss for words All his dreams, hopes and ambitions were being completed in one go, yet there was a sacrifice. Unfortunately, it would be dear Zesty bhai who would be the sacrificial lamb.

He thought of all the years of unselfishness, kindness and generosity Zesty bhai had brought to the whole of Bradford and maybe throughout the world. Unfortunately, the community was very disappointed.

"I understand this is not what you were expecting, however, brother Marpuf who grills chicken at Blando's every day, has a plot of land in Rutta, Pakistan. It is just enough to build a house, a lovely garden and a parking for two vehicles. He wants to donate it to you free of charge, for your kindness and representation of the community, which due to the possession of this land and your wife's origin will give you good stead to become a legal, upright and honourable Pakistani citizen. Bhai Ali has many contacts in the embassy, and he will arrange all the necessary paperwork."

"But doesn't Marpuf bhai have some kind of mental health issue?" Asked a confused Raja.

"Well, not anymore, as he is taking his medication and stopped drinking too. He is also not seeing jinn's anymore. What do you say sir?" Questioned Zubair, in a lowered tone.

Raja Walid Zindabad thought for one moment, and in one sentence without drawing a breath, while raising his head in his iconic arrogant style, said in an indignant tone, "Astaghfirullah, this so-called imam has betrayed us all, he has made a mockery of the community, our religion, respect and the future of our beloved masjid. I will speak to him immediately."

There was chanting in the background.

Raja Walid Zindabad!

Raja Walid Zindabad!

Raja Walid Zindabad!

"Thank you so much for understanding our plight. You are a gentleman and a scholar." Said Zubair
He stood up and everybody embraced him.
The Still Dre song played in his mind.
As he left the building, Raja Walid Khan Zindabad, gazed up at the night sky, thinking of his ignorant ancestors and whispered to himself, "I broke the curse."
As he left the Prayer hall, he looked up again at the sky and smiled. He put his arms into the air as though he was about to catch an angel falling out of the sky. A slight patter of rain fell onto his face, he spun round and round in a slow motion with a huge smug grin.
Now, he was a boss, a proper Pakistani, an OG as the youngers would say. But first he had to do his newfound duty, his first duty for his motherland, Pakistan. He had to betray one of his closest friend, Imam Zesty Bhai Hakim.

The two close old friends met, greeted each other, prayed together and then sat down together on the floor of the prayer hall in the Mosque.

"B-brother Hakim," stuttered Walid.

"What is it?" Asked Zesty with concern as he had never heard Brother Walid sound so nervous.

"It must be quite serious, as you haven't said any words of wisdom for a while and you keep referring to me as Hakim, I have a strange feeling that something really bad has happened." Said Zesty in a very serious tone.

"No matter what it is, I have so much love for you in my heart. You will always be my brother and most trusted friend, so speak freely, may Allah swt loosen your tongue and make everything easy for you, Inshallah."

"Well, I have been ordered by the community to speak with you about a delicate matter." Raja Walid Zindabad took a deep breath and all he could think about was the free land, his lifetime dream, and his Pakistani citizenship status. He then went on in a most assertive tone, to explain how badly let down the community had felt by him, betrayed and broken by his claim to self-promotion and publicity at the sacrifice and detriment of the Madrasa and the community. He continued explaining that they want him to leave his post with immediate effect. Raja Walid was so consumed by greed and blind ambition it had not occurred to him for one second that this would leave Zesty Bhai homeless. However, this would also allow the tight-fisted Raja to live in the Madrasa for free and he would be paid for the privilege.

Zesty bhai sighed deeply, looked up at his creator and asked for forgiveness for failing him and the community. As tears trickled down his face, he looked at his startled brother, put his hand on his knee and asked for forgiveness.

"Very well, I will pack my things immediately, please tell the congregation I am sorry for letting them down so badly." Said Zesty bhai.

"Furthermore, I hope and pray that the Imam after me will do a better job than I, brother. Please stay around and help and support him with the same kindness and devotion that you have shown me over the years. Promise me, my dearest brother." Whispered the saddened Imam. A very silent Raja felt shame, humiliation and he felt like the worst human being at what had just transpired. The truth and the betrayal of his heinous act had just hit him to the core.

So much for Brotherhood, I hear you say, just wait and see what lies ahead!

What had he done?

Imam Raja Walid Zindabad left the Madrasa with a numbness he had not experienced and stood outside. The world around him started spinning at an alarming rate. He looked up towards the sky and all he could see were dark clouds with the shape of smiling demonic faces.

He knew in his soul, the one he had just sold, that he would never be the same again He knew he had lost the tiny bit of happiness he had in his life and he also knew at that moment he would be in darkness until his demise. He felt his soul wretched in turmoil. He was disgusted with himself, yet his burning ambition, his final attempt at winning against Talar Shaliff was the ultimate prize.

He looked up towards the sky again, raised his fist and shouted angrily, "Where are you now Talar? I, Raja Walid have won. Who is the Pakistani Now?"

He knew Shaynaz would never forgive him. A darkness and a dull pain entered his heart for the first time in his existence. It did not even feel like this when his parents gave him away. He shook his head vigorously to say that the Imam had no reason to ask for forgiveness, but no words came out of his mouth.

This was the needle in the camel's haystack, the one that would break Raja Walid into 1000's of pieces, similar to Zesty bhai's jigsaw puzzles. But for this incident, he would never be able to put the pieces back together again.

Imam Zesty Bhai being a simple, humble man packed all his world's possessions into a single large suitcase. He wheeled the suitcase out of the madrasa, his home. As he left the building, Zesty bhai did not look back.

As soon as he was out of the building of his former home, he wept like a child, trying to hold back his emotions, tears ran down his face in a procession. He was alone and vulnerable and had left the mosque in disgrace. He remembered a saying, 'the road to hell is full of good intentions.' Suddenly without warning, the bulb started to flicker at the entrance to the Madrasa, it then went out, leaving the entrance to the Madrasa in quite dim. Zesty Bhai made his way to the local bed and breakfast with Callum and Mozzy, who had to leave the mosque immediately on the request of the general secretary of the mosque due to the bad publicity of being arrested.

As they arrived at the bed and breakfast, they all looked lost. They had no money, baggage or even food on them. Zesty bhai walked slightly ahead of them into the reception.

"We are all together," he said before the pair had a chance to speak.

They entered the small bed and breakfast with a numbness at the shock of what they had just endured, betrayed by the ones whom they trusted, broken by losing their homes, broke as they had no money and bald due to their genes. Zesty Bhai was fortunate enough to have a suitcase with him with clothing and his sweet memories. Luckily, Jamal had saved everything on a laptop for him, so he could look at his pictures and memories whenever he wanted to. Callum and Moscat had no belongings, just the clothes that they were wearing.

"Sunt ființe umane ca noi, unii dintre ei sunt de religii păgâne, care au nevoie de educație și unii par rătăciți, indiferent de starea lor au nevoie de ajutorul și sprijinul nostru." Said Mamica, to her daughters. *("They are human beings like us, some of them are of pagan religion, that need to be educated and some look lost Regardless of their condition, they need our help and support.")*

"Voi amândoi sunteți binecuvântarea și blestemul meu, ce pot face cu voi amândoi. Întâmpinați Vă oaspeții noștri, vă rog, cu puțină fericire, măcar să prefaceți. Când eram mare, nu îndrăznim să ne comportăm atât de nepoliticos." Ranted Mamica. (*You both are my blessing and my curse, what can I do with you both? Welcome our guests, please, with a little happiness, at least pretend. When we were growing up, we didn't dare to be so rude.*)

"Scuzați-mă, stimată doamnă a acestui bun stabiliment. Eu și prietenii mei suntem foarte recunoscători pentru amabilitatea și ospitalitatea ta fantastică. Dumnezeu să te binecuvânteze mereu pe tine și casa ta cu prosperitate și fericire." Said Zesty bhai directly to Mamica Olivia in his usual soft tone. *(Excuse me, dear lady of this good establishment. My friends and I are very grateful for your kindness and fantastic hospitality. May God always bless you and your home with prosperity and happiness.)*

The three ladies just froze, jaws dropped and stared directly at the unusual dark-skinned man with a priestly robe, a green turban and the ability to speak Romanian fluently. Now, Mamica had seen everything, she was not sure if she was dreaming or awake.

Hello, Hello, welcome. Please take a seat in the reception area, I will be with you shortly. In the meantime, can I get you guys some tea or coffee?" Asked Amelia, hurriedly with a huge grin on her face.

Mamica for once was completely lost for words, her whole face turned red. Eva was smiling thinking how interesting the next few days were going to be.

They all settled into their room. Unfortunately, Callum and Mozzy had to share a room as there were no other rooms available. Zesty had his own room as he was paying. However, he as a gentleman and a scholar offered his room to them both, but they declined as they both felt ashamed and humbled to depths they had never experienced before.

They all had dinner together; Callum was staring at Mozzy and Mozzy was staring at Callum with nothing but demonic thoughts zooming through their minds for each other since they had to push out their hatred and anger on something or someone. Zesty forever the optimist, spoke in Romanian to Mamica, nonstop, like a child who just made a new best friend. In his soft tone, he asked her all about her life and told her how amazing she was. She had created a beautiful life by herself and how brave she was to emigrate to a new country and asked her where and how did she find the strength. Mamica had never really spoken to someone apart from her daughters in her mother tongue since she came to England. Both Zesty and Mamica really got on, especially when Zesty followed her into the kitchen and helped her clean up whilst listening intently to all the things she had to endure after her beloved Florin passed. She cried, laughed and talked nonstop even after they had cleared up. She reminded him of his beloved so much. As he listened to her talk, he could not help but miss his congregation.

In the morning, they all got up early, though Zesty got up earlier than everyone and after praying and being grateful for a roof over his head, he helped Mamica make breakfast. He told so many jokes to her and asked her if she believed in god. She told him that she was devoutly religious and only read the bible in Latin. Zesty was very impressed and asked if she would read the bible to him in Latin.

Mamica was so delighted, she ran over to the cupboard, got out her huge leather bound and old bible and started reading it to him. Zesty was listening intently, he realised that he loved listening to her voice.

Aunty Shaynaz had been contemplating for the last few years whether or not she should adopt or foster a kid. She so dearly wanted children, a family, a home full of laughter and she finally made her mind up to adopt. She plucked up the courage and sat down with her kind, considerate and loving husband and in a soft voice said, "My darling, our home is so silent, god has a different calling for us and this calling is full of blessings."

"Yes my dear, please go on," replied Imam Raja Walid Khan.

"Well, what I'm saying is, I think we should adopt two children. I have them in mind and have gone to see them both quite a few times. They have managed to steal my heart, so full of beauty and are so desperate to be loved." Aunty Shaynaz continued.

"Oh, how delightful, I bet a nice, beautiful brother and sister from Pakistan, yes?" Asked Raja.

Aunty Shaynaz smiled and replied, "No, not quite, however, we are all created by the almighty as equals, they are Muslim, I have a picture; would you like to see?" Asked Shaynaz, sheepishly.

She pulled out about 12 pictures of a small five- and six-year-old brother and sister.

Raja Walid Khan turned a slight grey colour, then a deep red, and then slowly started shaking with rage. His heinous betrayal of Zesty was torturing his soul, he was constantly feeling dizzy and feverish. It seemed as though a grey cloud followed him around, removing any type of happiness or contentment.

He started to go off the handle and snapped at everyone at the slightest of things. His stress levels reached an all-time and he was now a changed man, slowly becoming a fiend, a monster. He was so enraged; he did not even notice the fear in his beloved wife's eyes. He did not even notice that her fear turned into strength and then anger, leading to hatred.

"Over my dead body! Is this some kind of a terrible joke? Have you lost your bloody mind, woman?! They are not allowed in my home!"

Shaynaz was a walking angel; In her adult lifetime she had never been spoken to like this by any person and got away with it, least of all her husband. As a child, it was a very different story as she had an extremely traumatic childhood.

In sheer shock, she froze, but a whimper escaped from her lips. She became a child in her mind again; the same child who was too afraid to stand up for herself from an oppressive upbringing and the very racist institution she had to endure

tiny voice came into her mind saying, 'You are not her anymore!'

"Why?" She asked in such a low whispered tone, it felt like she had just made a mouth movement yet hardly anything came out.

"Because, you blithering idiot, they are black!" Raja Walid shouted at the top of his voice. "I will become a laughing stock! The answer is no! And that's final. Never bring this conversation up again!" He said.

All of a sudden, she felt powerful. She stood up and stared straight at this stranger, whom she no longer knew.

"Yes!" She shouted back, regained her composure and continued, "Yes they are black, the same colour as the ink of the words written in the holy Quran, the same colour as the first man to give the Adhan (Islamic call to prayer). They are children! Babies who don't have anybody in this world,. Yet they raise their hands and bow their heads down to Allah swt with nothing but gratitude and love. Why don't you meet them once? I'm sure your heart will melt, as mine does each time they give me salaam. The whole community will respect you, not laugh at you!" Said Shaynaz with what seemed to be some kind of possession, as she had never spoken to her husband so defiantly.

"NO! NO! NO! If you bring this matter up again, I will divorce you tonight!" Yelled Raja Walid Khan.

"Then let it be. You will not last five minutes in this community without me! Whether you accept it or not, I will adopt these two children, in fact, I have already started the paperwork." Said an enraged Shaynaz.

"Get out of my house! You are a wicked, evil woman! That is why god did not give you any children." Retaliated her husband in anger.

"I thought deep down you were a kind Muslim man waiting to come out and change, to show your real self. The one that is kind and loving, the one whose heart would be filled with joy. Instead, the truth is that you are just a racist, like most of the bigoted so-called Muslim men out there. After all the racism you have endured throughout your life, how could you be this way? You are a cold hearted, vindictive and despicable man! You care only for what people will think, rather than the happiness and blessings you will receive by pleasing Allah swt. Furthermore, you are so wrong, Allah swt has given me two children and he will give me many, many more. It is you and you alone, he has not given children to!" She blurted out, without feeling any regret.

"Talaak!" (I divorce thee!) Her husband roared out, angrily.

Thunder struck, followed by a bolt of lightning, directly outside the house and it felt like the house was shaking.

Then there was a moment of silence between the two giant personalities of Bradford. Aunty Shaynaz did not break down in tears, neither did she scream or cry hysterically.
 "No! You get out of my house, YOUR house was burned down. This is my house. I bought it to rent it out as an investment for our future, with all of my own money. Remember? So, you get out!" She yelled at him.

Then all her emotions came flooding out.

"I will never forgive you for betraying that dear, sweet, angel beloved Imam of ours. You remember him, don't you? The one person who stood by you when the whole community rejected you. The one who put you on the map, the one who was your only true friend. You remember that, don't you? That he was also a black man. Do you seriously think you could ever replace such a angel in our community?

How 'LOW' will you go to be accepted as a Pakistani? Why not just be happy to be a British?" She asked.

"It is only a matter of time before they replace you too! Our community bickers and hates each other with deeper passion than you could possibly understand. They are always at each other's throats, and it will always be like that. The Imam kept everyone together at peace as one ummah. What in the god's name have you done you blithering idiot, you imbecile! All hell will break loose, and then they will all turn on you as they need someone to blame. How could you have been so naive? Do you even realise that you have been used and groomed for their own agenda. No matter how much good that man has done, no matter how much kindness he has shown, this racist community could not accept that he was a black man as that is all that they see. GOD IS WATCHING YOU AND YOUR DESPICABLE ACTIONS!" Screeched an incensed Shaynaz.

"LOW, enough to marry you!" retorted Walid recklessly as pathetically he could think of nothing else to say.

"So go to your precious community, and live at the Madrasa. Go! Just get out! I don't ever want to see your face again!" She yelled.

As Shaynaz stared at the pictures of the kids, her eyes betrayed her and tears streamed down her face, and her heart started to sink into the depths of loneliness.

"There it is, a juncture of defiance, anger and consequence, leading to permanent life changing decisions." Sonam said in an earnest voice.

Sonam became silent, as a customer came and ordered an espresso to go.

Sonam continued as soon as the barista came back and rejoined her, "The thing is as far as relationships go, if nobody ever has an argument, either someone is lying or when a quarrel does take place it usually escalates from triviality to full scale wars."

Sonam felt a little kick in her belly, she sipped some more of her Mocha, rubbed her tummy then whispered a little prayer and continued her tale. The Barista asked if she was okay, and his young son rubbed her hand for comfort.

-Chapter 4-

<u>The Husbands</u>
<u>(Are always the last to know.)</u>

Aunty Shaynaz was now a force to be reckoned with, she was an unstoppable tornado. She arranged a meeting with Sonam, Maria, Sam, Samia and Hamzah at the local Kokni Cafe, as this was a solution to what seemed to become a huge issue that would cause irreparable damage to the delicacies of these two families. So, damage limitation needed to be implemented with immediate effect.

"I have called you all here as these two families are about to self-destruct. Nobody wants to be a grown up and resolve it. This is why I have called you all here. You will have to swear to secrecy." Said Shaynaz.

"Samia, if everybody agrees, are you happy to marry Hamzah? Can you see a future with him?" she asked sternly.

"As Allah wills." Samia replied diplomatically.

"That's all very well and proper, however, the question needs to be asked is, do you have any feelings for this young man?" Continued Shaynaz.

Samia lowered her gaze and slowly nodded her head to say yes, much to Hamzah's delight.

"Ok ood, he is a brave and kind young man." Said Shaynaz gently.

"Maria, are you happy to support this marriage?" Asked Shaynaz, turning towards Maria.

"Yes, of course e is perfect for her, and I know he will always love and support her." Replied Maria.

"Mrs. Shakespeare " Said Shaynaz in a very serious tone.

"Sam, please call me Sam." Sam answered hastily.

"Okay, Sam, are you happy to support this marriage?" Asked Shaynaz gently.

"Yes, of cours Whatever makes the kids happy is fine by me. I do worry about how young and vulnerable they are though. Maybe they should live a little first." Said Sam whilst rubbing her chin. "But, who am I to stand in the way of love? Some of us just read or dream of it." She continued.

"Sonam Beti, are you happy about this marriage going ahead?" Asked Shaynaz in a lowered tone.

"Yes, defo Aunty. I already know how many outfits she will wear, and have decided her different makeup and hair styles and I have his entire attire lined up." Said Sonam as a matter of factly, in a very animated voice.

All the ladies burst out into laughter, including the blushing Samia and a very in love Hamzah.

"Okay, great." Answered a very satisfied Aunty Shaynaz.

"Hamzah, all the women agree with this marriage to go ahead. So, you two suitors have our full support. The problem lies with the men in this family, who are al-" Before Aunty Shaynaz could even finish her sentence, they all blurted out their thoughts.

"Backwards," yelled Maria.

"Stubborn," shouted Sonam.

"Fat losers," shrieked Sam.

"Bigots," said Aunty Shaynaz, not wanting to be left out.

"Lost," shouted Hamzah as that was all he could think of at the time.

All the co-conspirators started laughing hysterically like a group of school kids.

"This is my plan." Shaynaz leaned in, then summoned them towards her and they all followed suit. In a very hushed tone, the plan was relayed to everyone.
"Hamzah, a very close friend of mine called Chah-Chah Pardroh is admittedly a very intelligent, good and a kind man. Unfortunately, he was quite egotistical, but nobody is perfect. He is in desperate need of some help at his homeless shelter. It is based in Birmingham and if your mum allows, I hope you will take up this offer. It is a paid position, and it includes board and lodgings for a month. Samia, a very old friend owns a residential home for old people in Scotland. She could really do with a bit of help and support at her place. It is a paid position as well and includes board and lodging too. If your mum allows you to go, it would be quite beneficial for all concerned until this thing gets resolved. Maria and Sam, I want you both to go and contact your respective husbands at the bed and breakfast and tell them you have received a text message from both Samia and Hamzah, saying that they have gone to India to meet Salman Khan, and ask him to take permission from your father for Hamzah to marry Samia. This gives time for the men in this family to get together and realise that the only thing that matters is the happiness of their children. Everything else seems irrelevant. This marriage is meant to be, and it will go ahead regardless of their prejudices, and they will have to either agree and be happy with it or just butt out." Aunty Shaynaz said and everybody looked at her with complete respect. "I think the love they

have for their children will out way any bigotry, racism and hate, as in my eyes love conquers all." Contined Aunty Shaynaz.

Due to the selfishness and obstinacy of the men in both families, they had never ever been given a chance to prove how much they actually loved their children and how far they would go to prove their fatherhood, especially as they felt let down by their own fathers so badly. Therefore, the scheming ladies and of course, young Hamzah simply assumed the hate filled men would:

- Get Angry.
- Sulk.
- Burp/Fart.
- Blame their respective partners.
- Sulk.
- Lash Out.
- Panic.
- Get Angry.
- Worry about the kids.
- Eat and Drink.
- Blame themselves.
- Blame their respective Partners.
- Get together.
- Sort out their differences.
- Blame Everyone.
- Feel Sorry for themselves.
- Find the kids.
- Burp/Fart.

- Realise they are fighting a losing battle.
- Put their differences aside.
- Start getting on.
- Agree to the marriages.
- Carry on as before.
- Never mention it again.

Quite predictable really.

Little did the conspirators know what would prevail. They also did not understand and underestimated the passion of a man. They did not comprehend that beneath all those hidden feelings for the last 50 odd years were similar to that of an uncaged tiger. This will become that definitive moment when they actually uncaged the tiger. A man's purpose is to protect, and to provide and this is his primal instinct. In modern times, this is almost obsolete along with the demise of the role of men, as women can now provide for themselves, have the police force to protect them and also have stalking laws.

"So, ladies you are all sworn to secrecy and Samia and Hamzah, you will have to stay off the internet for at least a month. It will give you both time to reflect and think about what you both want to do in your future. She then asked for both of their phones and gave them some old phones and a charger with no cameras on them.
"They are both live. Please tap in your mothers' and everyone present in this room, phone numbers. We are your only point of contact. You must go right now, I have a taxi and train

tickets booked for you both. One to Scotland and the other to Birmingham. I have also taken the liberty of contacting the Chief constable and told them Hamzah and Samia are not missing or in India and for their safety and well-being, I have relocated them to the addresses where you will be staying at, so if there's any issue, she will be your emergency contact." Shaynaz said. From under the table, she rolled out two shiny silver metallic suitcases. Both of them had a tag, each, with their names on them.

"I have packed some toiletries and some Islamic clothing which should fit you both. I have booked you both taxis that will be waiting for you at the stations and have also booked a taxi to get you both to the station. Your taxi is waiting outside, both of you can say your goodbyes on your way to the station. Unfortunately, once you reach the station, you will be going in opposite directions. Here are two prepaid credit cards, on each card there is £1500 and here is a further £500 in cash".

Aunty Shaynaz then gave each of them brown envelopes containing everything.

"Between us all, we can top up if you need more. You are not allowed to contact anyone else, this means no one apart from who is at this table, do you understand?" Asked Aunty Shaynaz. The two youngster's both nodded.

"You can both talk to each other every day." Said Aunty Shaynaz.

Samia looked scared, whereas, Hamzah looked shocked, but they both nodded in agreement.

Aunty Shaynaz had gotten every angle covered, nobody could see fault with the plan, it seemed perfect.

"After month, all of this will be sorted out and you guys can return. The wedding will then take place and you will live happily ever after." Aunty Shaynaz reassured the couple.

They all hugged each other and watched as the two young adults entered the taxi.

They all sat back down, and tears trickled down Maria's face which triggered Aunty Shaynaz and Sam. Where there was laughter only a few moments earlier, it was now replaced by a painful, empty sadness.

"Omg," said Maria and Sam in unison.

"You cannot pay for all this. The fact that you had such a wonderful idea is enough. Give me your bank details, and I will put in two thousand towards it all." Said Sam.

"Yes, great idea! I will put in the other two grand, and before you get offended, just know that the fact you took care of everything including your contacts, employment, taxis, travel and accommodation, is more than enough." Sam joined in.

Just then Sonam's phone started ringing, breaking the silence.

"Yes. Okay. Okay. I'm on my way, No! No! No! Do not try and set the stand up, you do not for the life of me, possess any technical skills. DO NOTHING! I am on my way." Sonam replied to someone on the other line.

She stood up and hugged the three older women.

"Everything will work out. I have full faith in my adorable Aunt." Yelled Sonam as she rushed off to fix another problem.

Samia settled in at the care home straight away and before even unpacking started to help out immediately. All who encountered the purity and kindness of Samia were all enchanted by her and the level of kindness that she naturally shared. They had not experienced it before; even from their own loved ones and dearest families. They would all happily tell her about their entire lives with what seemed like for the first time ever. Samia in return would listen intently, laugh at the fun times and would hold their hands while they explained the sad bits of their lives and when they got teary eyed, she would secretly be glad as it would keep her busy and keep her mind from wandering. She would pray at night, and then later call Hamzah. They would talk for hours on end until one of them fell asleep. They both counted the days when they could return home. They were looking forward to the wedding and decided to keep it small and spend the left over amount from their budget on feeding the homeless, poor and needy as a perfect wedding feast. She was starting to miss him, and she allowed her heart to finally open up. She fell head over heels in love with Hamzah, The Brave (شجاع Shujae) . Whenever she thought back, she realised he had always been there for her, always supporting all her endeavours, and never asking for anything in return. She could not wait to be married to him. Strangely, even though he was always with her, it never entered her mind that she would never not have him in her life. Them being apart now, made her realise how significant and supportive he was. She felt a twang of guilt when she realised that she may have taken him for granted. It also made her feel quite naive.

Hamzah was totally blown away as he really enjoyed living in Birmingham. Although he ached to be with his beloved Samia every minute of the day and looked forward to speaking to her every night as it was the only thing that kept him going. He was constantly texting her day and night to be up to date with her life as though he was right next to her and not three hundred and fifty miles away. His work kept him busy, and he met a lot of reverts, brothers and sisters from seemingly every part of the globe. They befriended him and took him in as a real brother. They also invited him around to their respective homes and he felt like he had a new family. He called everyone brother or sister and he strangely experienced and felt a sense of belonging. His newfound god given family loved teaching him all the beauty of Islam. He did a lot of volunteer work in the name of Allah and perfected his prayers. He became a bit of a superstar at his new local Madrasa as he was always there in his spare time, offering a helping hand He sat with the elders, and they would talk to him for hours on end, often wishing they had a son or even a son in law with the same respect, morals and values he showed them. What was quite ironic was that they would pray for Hamzah's parents and bless them for bringing up such a good boy.

His favourite food in Birmingham was a good Balti Chicken Tikka Masala with lots of chillies, pickles and poppadom's with a family naan. He used to tell Samia about it and she could not believe he was able to eat the whole lot by himself. She giggled herself to sleep sometimes as he was talking to her. He missed her like the desert missed the rain. He became friends with a young beautiful lady called Ellz at the local chip shop, she was Greek Cypriot and was the daughter of the owner of the shop. It was called Chris's Fish Bar and was established in 1970 it had won many awards and used to have huge queues on a weekend, Hamzah used to help out sometimes when it got really busy. He used to tell her all about Samia all the time. Ellz thought it was so romantic, how much he would talk about his future wife.

Now just to clarify, Callum, & Mozzy had four things in common:

1. They did not believe in putting any money into the greedy banks. One did not want to pay his taxes as he did not want to fund Shariah Law, and the other did not want to pay his taxes as he thought he had worked for it; therefore, it was his and he had already given enough. They both kept their cash at home under their respective beds. This was the safest place to put it as it was always close to them.

2. They were both born and bred in Bradford, Great Britain & were avid Man City fans (season ticket holders, thank you very much).

3. They were both abandoned by their respective fathers at a very tender age.

4. They would never abandon their children under any circumstances.

-Chapter 5-

Blame the Tool!

After a lifetime of hatred for each other's races the two ignorant gentlemen ended up sharing a room together. They had no money, no friends, and had just been dumped by their respective partners. They were homeless and facing criminal charges due to what transpired as the explosion may have been their fault and the pair were in a state of shock. The future looked bleak, it was literally impossible to rebuild your life at 50, starting from scratch. It was like a recurring nightmare that would not end. They both felt that it was imperative to show primal dominance and be comfortable enough to fart and belch in the room until their hearts were content, alongside snoring and talking in their sleep. They passed their time indulging in racist slurs and general mick taking, aimed at each other.

"Why do you keep wobbling your head when you talk?" Enquired Callum with a straight face.

"The same reason you smell of curry on a Friday night." Said a sullen Mozzy.

"If you love Islam, why not move to Meccastan?" Said Callum with a glare.

"Can you please tell the Royal family to return the huge diamond on the queen's crown back to India?" Said Mozzy with a slightly pompous attitude.

"Why do you keep grooming innocent kids?" Asked Callum.

"Why did you murder, rape, rob and pillage almost half the globe and then call yourself, 'Great Britain?" Asked Mozzy.

Both of their wives had taken the liberty of moving into hotels in the next town as they had been wise enough to secretly save and invest all of their income streams whilst leaching off their husbands hard earned money, that they had ever made, which left them quite wealthy, and able to afford very expensive hotels and solicitors who now offered their services to serve their now ex-husbands divorce papers.

Mozzy and Callum could not understand how a man they did not know paid for their board and lodgings with so much love from his heart, and without expecting a single thing in return. He gave them some Islamic robes to get changed into, and also ensured they received a bag full of toiletries which turned out to be a lifesaver. He even told the staff at the bed and breakfast to give them whatever they asked for and not to ask them for a single penny. The great Imam insisted he would pay for everything whilst they stayed here as his guests. They only found this out, as every time they were offered something, they refused as they were penniless, the staff simply smiled and told them that the imam had already paid for it. What really baffled the gentlemen was that he did not ask them for anything personal apart from if they were hungry. He even ordered food for them when he heard them complaining about craving fish and chips.

Who was this amazing man they thought.

They were forced to have nothing but complete respect for this angelic being. Eventually, after a few excruciating days, Callum finally admitted that not all Muslamics were bad people, and in return Mozzy admitted that he just wanted to be accepted as a real Yorkshire man as he did not know any other way of life apart from the British way of life. He was humbled by the fact that a stranger was so kind to them without asking them a single question or any kind of prejudice. He finally understood why his Uncle Walid was always with this man

Strangely, Moscat had never spoken to him before. The man, which Callum now knew as Zesty, sat with him every night and asked if there was anything else he could do to make his life easier. Callum was in a state of questioning everything he had ever known, been taught and told. What bewildered him so much was the fact that not a single patriot had come to his rescue or had come to help or even offer a hand in friendship. Zesty without a doubt was the best person he had ever met. He was a black Muslamic, so Callum was supposed to hate with a vengeance. and Instead, he felt drawn to him with faith and trust as you would an older brother, he felt at peace whenever he was nearby. He had never endured this level of kindness in his life. Callum started asking Zesty about the Muslamic religion. All the questions had a lot of anger and hate filled innuendos, yet Zesty answered each one with a huge smile, love and kindness in his soft calming voice. The three of them often played monopoly together, this Zesty felt gave the pair their self-respect back giving them both purpose and something to look forward to creating a deep bond of togetherness, so at this time of their lives they did not feel alone and the fact that they were both businessmen who needed inspiration. The kindness that they were shown inspired the pair to help around the bed and breakfast so they did not feel like they were nothing but a pair of sad scrounging men or a charity case. Callum and Mozzy for the first time in their lives, started speaking to one another in the darkness of the night, about their whole life in detail. It turned out, their lives were almost identical, and they started to build an unbreakable bond and a lifetime of friendship. Yet they were both absolutely clueless about what was about to happen in the next chapter of their lives.

Both the absent fathers received the text on their individual handsets with exactly the same message, at the same time.

'YOU ARSEHOLE OF A LOSER! BECAUSE OF YOUR PIG HEADED AND STUBBORNLY PATHETIC ATTITUDE, OUR BEAUTIFUL CHILD HAVE RUN OFF TO INDIA, TO GET THE BLESSINGS OF MR. SALMAN KHAN SO THEY CAN GET HIS PERMISSION TO GET MARRIED!!! FIX THIS!!! DO SOMETHING GOOD IN YOUR LIFE FOR ONCE!

P.S. SIGN THE DIVORCE PAPERS, YOU ARE GROSS AND YOU SMELL!!!'

To the absolute horror of the two avid MCFC fans, they were duty bound fathers. They went into primal mode and all they could think of was to protect their offspring they reacted in the only way they knew how and that was an act of ill thought out spontaneity, they had to get on a plane fast, their respective children had gone to India, to seek the blessings of Salman Khan.
They had really messed up and handled everything horribly, and this was their redemption.
They both looked at each other.
Where do they even start?

Callum rang up Uncle Joey, and Mozzy rang up his only contact, Sonam.
Within 30 minutes Sonam, Uncle Joey and Taylor turned up at the bed and breakfast.
"What the hell is going on?" Asked Uncle Joey.
"It's the k-k-kids." Stuttered Callum.
"Huh?" Questioned a confused Taylor.
"They have eloped and run off to bloody India, ain't it?" Shouted Mozzy.
"We need to go now, before it's too late and something happens to them!" Said Callum.
"How?" Asked Mozzy.
"Leave it to me," said Sonam. "I will arrange for emergency passports, and a flight to Mumbai. I have a credit card".
"Me too," shouted Taylor.
"Looks like we are going to Pakistan, then!" Uncle Joey said.

"INDIA! THEY ARE BOTH IN MUMBAI!" They all shouted at a bewildered Joey, simultaneously.

Meanwhile in the new found freedom of Maria's world.
Maria texted Christian and said it was over between her and her husband and she could really do with a friend to talk to. Christian asked where she was and reached there in thirty minutes flat. Maria was about to seal the fate of her now collapsed marriage. She did not once consider her own dignity, religion, respect, marriage or her family. All she craved was to be loved and treated like the beautiful queen that she was.

Christian met her in the hotel reception, they had a cup of coffee and talked for hours, well actually it was Maria who kept talking, mainly about how she longed to be held and loved mentioning how powerful and feminine she felt when dancing with Christian. She droned on about hiw much she hated being married to HIM and was relieved it was all over.
Christian got up and sat next to her staring intently into her eyes.
Christian just listened and nodded a lot, this went on into the night. All the time that Maria was talking all Christian could think of was at what stage should he say lets go to your room and how to get her PIN number. The hotel staff started to clean up and hinted that it was time to close. They both went upstairs to Maria's room, and they became intimate, making love all night. Maria had never experienced anything like this in her entire life, she had only read about it in the romantic novels she read as a teenager. Maria fell head over heels in love with Christian. They spent every night and day together. Christian was always on the phone arguing with his family back in Brazil. She was finally happy, he was so attentive and came across as genuine, unbelievably handsome so she took the plunge and offered him a business partnership in all of her business affairs, so, they could become one. Unfortunately, it turned out that Christian did not live up to his name and was already married and the arguments he was always having were with his wife in Brazil. He gained complete trust from the very smart yet unbelievably trusting and naive Maria and cleaned out all of her savings, shares, stocks, bonds and cryptocurrency and went back to Brazil as a very married, wealthy man.

Maria could not cope. What had she done? She lost everything over a fling. How could she have been so stupid? The caveman would have never betrayed her. She had a nervous breakdown and was sectioned into the local mental institution. She became obsessed with dancing all night and ranting and raving about her lost funds, whilst scratching herself red and raw all over her body as the stress bought her out in a rash. She never thought for one moment of karma. She had betrayed Mozzy at his lowest point, and in return she was betrayed at what she thought was her highest point.

Sam started to look at really expensive apartments in Mayfair and registered with Shakespeare's Property to find a place with immediate effect. On her first visit there, she was overwhelmed by all the glitz and glamour of London, it was all she had ever dreamed of. She moved into an apartment and outside the building, she met him. She felt like this is how Lady Diana must have felt when she met Dodi. It was a love at first sight. He was coming out of his blue Rolls Royce, and they stood less than a foot away from each other. She forgot to breathe, as they stared into each other's eyes. He was tall, dark, handsome, rich and mysterious with jet black piercing eyes and a fantastic torso to match. She spent a whole week with him, visiting glamorous places in the capital, staying at luxurious hotels and eating at fancy restaurants. This was her moment, everything she had ever dreamed of.

He opened a beautiful salon for her on Oxford St. in central London. What more could she ask for? The world was at her feet and so was Arkhmed.

He went down on one knee and proposed to her, she accepted immediately. She did explain that technically she was still married to sir 'Fart a lot'. He responded by telling her that it was not a problem as they will get married in his home country, Egypt. It was apparently allowed to be married to multiple people at the same time without an issue. The problem was unbeknownst to Sam, she would become his wife number four.

-Chapter 6-

Jolly Good to Bollywood

Hindustan Times

Bollywood Actor Salman Khan,

Who was sentenced to five years' jail term in the 20-year-old blackbuck case, was prisoner No. 106 in Jodhpur Central Jail on Thursday night and was lodged in the barrack next to Asaram Bapu's. With his bail plea reserved for Saturday, he is expected to stay in jail for at least another night. The actor ate a simple dinner of dal, sabzi and chapatis and slept on the floor. He refused breakfast on Friday morning.

Also in India, the very famous chef, Anstey Harlot was looking forward to his cooking around India tour. He had a film crew at the ready. He had a specially adapted entertainers travel bus with the most spectacular kitchen you would ever see. His first stop was at Filmistan Studios, where he was not only cooking up a treat for a famous director, but he was also going to be one of the judges at a Salman khan lookalike competition. He loved going to India as he was able to get real natural ingredients straight from the root and was able to cook like a local. He knew the UK television viewers would lap it up. Judging by all the positive messages he constantly received from his huge fan base on his various social media channels, he felt he was very welcomed in India.

Anstey was going over scripts and recipes when all of a sudden, the bus released a very loud bang, shuddered and came to a grinding halt. Everybody clambered off the bus and saw the smoke coming out of the engine. Harlot was not happy to say the least as now he would be late; he was used to always being on time. The crew called a number of people, unfortunately, nobody could get to them until at least four hours later. They all sat in the bus and could do nothing but wait in the baking heat. They had a few cases of ice-cold beer and some cheese and tomato paninis, so they were having a great time while waiting for the rescue team. Anstey's mobile suddenly rang.

"Hello, hello?" Said Anstey Harrlot's agent.

"Hello, mate, how is it looking?" Answered a man from the other side.

"We've got some good news! A group of dancers who are also on tour, are heading your way on a coach. Apparently, they are quite unique and already well-known in India. They will make a stop where you are. The driver has been instructed to pick you and your crew up. Luckily, they are also heading to Filmistan Studios to perform." Said the agent.

"Mate what a stroke of luck!" Beamed Harrlot. "How long before they get here?" He asked in a very chirpy and optimistic tone.

"A few hours, so not too long. Hang tight and look out for them," said the agent.
"Okay, lovely. Ciao."said Anstey.

The anxious and stressed-out families landed at Chhatrapati Shivaji Maharaj International Airport in Mumbai, without any luggage and got through customs quickly. They knew due to their google searches that Salman Khan may be at Filmistan studios. It mentioned his name and that is all they had to go on.

Meanwhile at the Dawa khana (local surgery).

श्री करम मालिह ने कहा, दयालु डॉक्टर, आपके पास कई मानसिक स्वास्थ्य समस्याएं हैं, आपके पास एक से अधिक व्यक्तित्व विकार और गंभीर सिज़ोफ्रेनिया है। सावधानीपूर्वक निरीक्षण के बाद आपके व्यक्तित्व आपसे यह सोचकर झूलते हैं कि आप भारत की रक्षा करने वाले ब्रिटिश साम्राज्य के खिलाफ युद्ध में हैं। आपको लगता है कि आप एक मेगा बॉलीवुड स्टार हैं और रूसी माफिया और गैंगस्टा रैपर के लिए एक गेटअवे ड्राइवर हैं। सौभाग्य से इस सब के नीचे एक सुंदर विनम्र लड़का है जो आप असली हैं। आप वास्तव में एक बहुत ही धन्य व्यक्ति हैं क्योंकि हमारे पास कुछ बहुत ही शक्तिशाली दवाएँ हैं। जब तक आप इन गोलियों को दिन में तीन बार लेते हैं, तब तक आप ठीक रहेंगे। कृपया टेबलेट लेने के 30 मिनट बाद तक भारी मशीनरी का संचालन न करें या वाहन न चलाएं और यदि आप इन नियमों का पालन करते हैं और उन पर

टिके रहते हैं तो पूरे भारत में किसी को भी आपकी स्थिति का अंदाजा नहीं होगा और आप वैसे ही विचारशील व्यक्ति बने रहेंगे जैसे आप हैं।
हालांकि अगर आप इन गोलियों को लेना भूल जाते हैं तो भगवान आपके साथ कमरे में मौजूद सभी लोगों की मदद करें।

(The kind doctor said to Mr Karam Maliyh) "You have multiple mental health issues, you have a multiple personality disorder and severe schizophrenia. After careful observation, your personalities swing from you hallucinating that you are in a war against the British Empire protecting India to you thinking that you are a mega Bollywood star and a getaway driver for the Russian mafia and a Gangster Rapper. Fortunately, underneath all of this is a kind-hearted humble guy who is the real you. You are indeed a very blessed man because we have some very strong medication. As long as you take these tablets three times a day, you will be fine. Please do not operate heavy machinery or drive a vehicle until 30 minutes after consuming the tablets and if you abide and stick to these rules, nobody in the whole of India will have any idea of your condition and you will remain the kind considerate man you are. However, if you forget to take these tablets god help whoever is in the room with you.")

The humble Taxi driver picked up the medication, put it into his shirt pocket and said, "thank you" and went into his jeep. He thanked God every day for Uber as it allowed him to work and support his family. Due to his condition, nobody would employ him so he used his initiative and became self employed His job and car were his pride and joy.

He drove towards the airport as the booking had been confirmed, he met the Khan and Shakespeare Clan at the airport, got them all on board and initially drove at a steady pace along the traffic polluted highways, and towards Filmistan Studios. The driver loved to practise his English at every available opportunity and as Uncle Joey was sitting next to him, he started discussing about what impact the UK had made on India during its 300 year reign. He also explained how well The East India Company had run India and they should never have left. The master race, the white men, the English gentlemen, were some of the best things that had ever happened to India, without a doubt.

Uncle Joey felt pride come over him as he remembered the time when The British Empire ruled almost all over the world. Unfortunately, as the journey was progressing, it turned out every time the humble driver went over a deep pothole, it would trigger one of his multiple personalities. The problem with this was that nobody including the driver knew which of his personality would come out, and to make things worse the driver suffered from hallucinations so when he flipped into a personality his surroundings changed into that particular hallucinogenic character.

"We are taking a small detour, I am just pulling up to the gentlemen's room, you are all free to do some shopping and use the facilities or buy some Indian street food. Please ensure you are back here in exactly thirty minutes," said the driver.

He felt very queasy and needed to take his medication at the first available opportunity as forewarned by the Doctor.

"Hang on matey, the studio is only thirty minutes away according to google maps so can you just keep on driving?" Said a very assertive and adamant Sonam.

"Madam ji, please try and understand, I really need the little boys' room, I cannot continue until I have gone there." Said the sweaty driver.
Uncle Joey was having none of it and grabbed the driver's shirt.
"Mate, either you take us to the studio right now or we take this vehicle with you in the boot!" Uncle Joey threatened the poor man. Unfortunately, the man's pack of medicine fell out and wedged itself in between the car
seat and the section where the seat belt goes, yes, you know the bit that nobody can get to.
The driver, scared out of his wits, agreed to get them to the studios as quickly as he could, without stopping. He
thought he would just pop a pill whilst he was driving, and nobody would even notice, so they continued on their journey. The driver fumbled around for his medication in the breast pocket of his shirt, yet could not locate his very strong and desperately needed medication. They accidentally went over a very large deep and very dusty pothole, jerking the whole car and causing the suspension to make a very loud and scary cranking noise.

The driver looked at himself in the rear-view mirror and saw a bright illuminating flash of light.

Suddenly, the car magically transformed into a huge limo with only him and Sonam in the car. He was driving and she was sitting right in the rear seat behind him blowing kisses and winking at him.

He stared straight at her and a very familiar tune started playing on the radio by the click of his fingers. Magically, disco lights were emitting rays of groovy light from the small ballroom globes and strobe lights.

He flicked his hair back with a quick jerk of his neck and smiled out of the corner of his mouth, looking quite smug and hot.

A Bollywood song called 'L O V E' from the olden days of disco started to blurt out the radio.

Madam ji shyly looked away and bit into the middle of her hooked finger.

As the driver sang to Madam ji, she stared straight into his eyes and mouthed *'I love you'* and blew him a kiss.

Everybody in the taxi started staring at the driver. They were a little concerned as to why the driver was twitching, mumbling stuff, and he did not seem to be paying much attention to the roads.

The driver pulled out a beautiful rose, he kept behind the visor. He breathed heavily on the screen of his limousine and drew a heart with the stem of the rose onto the steamed screen and handed it to madam ji. She accepted it in between her teeth and joined in singing with him. Leaning over and wrapping her arms around the headorest and tilting her head slightly side to side with nothing but love in her eyes.

The driver, now increasing the speed of the vehicle, went above another pothole and a flashing light beamed from the rear-view mirror, almost blinding him.
The car went pitch black and the vehicle started to slow down to a very slow speed, the driver started to stare at Uncle Joey and moving his head up and down in a very slow gangster style head rocking motion. He tightened his eyes and put his hand inside his shirt just below his chest as though he was about to pull out a gun.
Suddenly, he clicked his fingers and a tune burst out of the radio.

Uncle Joey turned around to look at others and said, "I'm not a shrink or anything but I think this guy has a screw loose."

The driver, hallucinating again, knew his homies in his car would be finding beef tonight He showed his gold teeth as he smiled, he was going gang banging tonight. He knew he could trust his boys, his krew.

"We should have let this guy go to the toilet; I think he is desperate to go pee. Hence, the strange twitching and grunting sounds." Said Mozzy.

The driver, even though he was going slowly, bounced over a severely deep pothole again and a bright light flashed from the rear-view mirror.

He was riding his chariot as fast as he could and was waving his swords, shouting in Hindi.

कमीनों, तुम्हारे पास कभी हमारी आत्मा या हमारा भारत नहीं होगा।

(You Bastards, you will never have our souls or our India.)

As the driver looked to his left, he saw a British soldier telling him that they were his masters, whilst pointing a rifle at him. He whipped the horses harder, making them pull the chariot as fast as a tornado.

Uncle Joey looked at the driver who was now twitching uncontrollably and to top it all off, his mouth was foaming. He had his mouth wide open and was groaning. Uncle Joey recognised these symptoms as a man who was desperate to go to the toilet.

"I agree, this guy is a trooper just to get us to our destination. He is enduring horrific pain by holding his piss back. I think let the guy pull over and relieve himself as he is driving like a nut job, we have narrowly missed about 4 cars, two trucks, a few random stray cows and a dog." stated Uncle Joey.

All of a sudden, the driver immediately turned left onto a dusty road. It had no markings and was bumpy. Even the jeep was rocking all over the place, the suspension was no longer doing its job.

The driver saw another illuminating bright light from the rear view mirror, and spoke in Russian.

"Вы, ублюдки, никогда не получите ни наших душ, ни нашей Индии."

(Do not worry comrade, we will lose these dogs and wait for them further up the highway and then gun them all down.)

He looked back at Callum and nodded in approval.
In reality, he just looked at Callum and mumbled some nonsense which was incomprehensible.
Callum looked at him and said, "I don't think this man is really here. Let's get this idiot to pull over and get him to relieve himself and put the poor guy out of his misery."

No sooner had they said this, the driver pressed the accelerator a little harder and started driving at a ferocious speed. Luckily, they could see other vehicles, which meant that there was civilisation nearby.

As they drove recklessly through a major highway and pot-holed terrain without adhering to any road laws whatsoever, they noticed a parked or possibly broken-down coach.
As they were driving on another endless highway, Taylor glanced up at a bus that seemed to have parked up. Suddenly, his life went into slow motion.
'Was it true?' He thought to himself and rubbed his eyes. Omg! He had to stop the driver by any means necessary.
"Pull over! Stop. Please Stop!" Shouted a hysterical Taylor. He started ranting and raving like a possessed man.

"STOP THE FREAKING CARRRRR!" Shouted Taylor.

He grabbed the driver and shook him into a frenzy. The driver snapped out of him morphing into someone else, for a second and then became a Bollywood movie star and started shouting with a most demonic look in his eyes, whilst driving at a very dangerous high speed.

"जो डरता है, वह मान लो कि वे पहले ही मर चुके हैं।"

(He who is afraid, assume that he is already dead).

Shouted the driver at the top of his voice and then did a proper villainous hysterical laugh, while looking up out of his window and started shooting his Kalashnikov towards the sky. The bullets sprayed upwards and let out a thunderous deafening noise.

"Look! Look! It's Anstey Harrlot s tour bus!" Said a hysterical Taylor, who was now frantically waving in the bus's direction. The driver drove towards the bus at a high speed and then slammed on the brakes with all his being, as he had to swerve past a stray cow, just missing the cow. They veered into the back of the tour bus, causing the entire vehicle to be crushed on one side. Luckily, they were all wearing their seatbelts, except the driver who went flying out through the front windscreen. Whilst he was flying through the air, the driver shouted out, *"Kitney Aadmi The!"* (How many men were there?) and then passed out midair. He miraculously landed on the back of the cow, which went all crazy and wild west buckaroo, kicking and jumping and ran off the highway, into a nearby field with an unconscious driver woho was completely oblivious to what was happening.

Taylor was starstruck and at a complete loss for words when he saw his idol asking him if he was okay. Was this another Anstey Harrlot dream of his? Was he hallucinating again?
He reached out his hand towards Anstey and said, "Is it really you?"
"Mate, are you okay? I am Anstey Harrlot, and we are looking after you and your friends." Anstey said and Taylor passed out in his arms.

Callum, Uncle Joey, Mozzy and Sonam were a bit shell shocked, but alright. They helped each other out of the wrecked car. Mozzy for the first time in Sonam's adult life saw a young innocent vulnerable girl who needed the strength of a father, not an ignorant dictator. He saw the reality of it all at his lowest. She sprang into action when he had nothing. She did not hesitate to pay for everything regardless of how he had treated her over the last few years. For the first time in his life, he was proud of his daughter, the one he looked at every day with disdain. The one he felt utterly disappointed with. So what if she never ever covered her head. So what if she did not become a doctor thought Mozzy. Now he saw her as a woman in her own right, a caring sister, a devoted daughter with the heart of a lioness and with kindness and compassion of a real angel.

'How misguided am I?' He thought, as he looked at her in awe. All these years he spent ignoring her and showing her how much of a disappointment she was. What the hell was he thinking? He then made a vow to himself to always give her the full respect she actually deserved and quite frankly had earned.

Anstey Harrlot was a kind and considerate man in real life, just as he was on the television. He asked all of them to come on board and offered them some ice-cold beer and some Samosas and Onion Bhajhis. The taxi was lodged into the side of the bus, blocking all access to any of the luggage that was in there.

They told their story of why they had come to India. Anstey and his television crew were all ears as the whole story sounded as though it had come straight out of a Bollywood script.

Anstey stood up and said, "Hang on me Old Mukka, did you guys say Salman Khan?"
"Salman Khan, the Bollywood actor. The most famous man in India?" Asked Anstey.
"Yes," replied Mozzy sheepishly.
"Oh my God, you will not believe this, e are on our way to meet Mr. Salman Khan at Filmistan Studio. Furthermore, another bus is coming to take us directly to Filmistan
Studios to specifically see Salman Khan. Mate what are the odds of that?"
They all looked at each other with feelings of jubilation and relief.

"Salman Can or Salman Can't, Cinderella shall go to the ball." Said Anstey with a can of beer in his hands.

About thirty minutes later, a huge bus pulled up next to Anstey's tour bus. The doors opened and a 6 feet, 3 inch, massive dark skinned muscular woman, wearing a sari clambered out of her tour bus and stood next to Anstey's bus and said,

"अरे लन्दन की हसीनाओं, चढ़ जाओ हमारी बस में, हम तुम्हारे सारे सपने सच कर देंगे।"

(Hey beauties of London, get on our bus, we will make all your dreams come true.)

Anstey hopped off the bus, followed by all the other passengers.

"Come on everybody we are saved. Hurray! " Cheered Anstey as he gestured for everyone to get onto the bus.
The All singing group of ladies were all fairly burly and quite masculine in appearance yet behaved as though they were shy, teenage newlyweds in saris. They started dancing and singing beautiful love songs in Hindi at the top of their voices. It was like a pantomime of some sort.

The driver of the bus had earphones in his ears and was talking to someone on the phone, so he was oblivious to all the singing, clapping and provocative dance moves.
Eventually they stopped singing, sat down and started to hand out savoury snacks and drinks. As soon as everyone finished eating and drinking, all the singing, clapping and dancing continued nonstop for another 25 minutes.
Eventually, when they stopped singing, the dancers asked them what they were all doing in India.

One of the ladies was fluent in English and would translate the whole story to the rest of the ladies. The ladies were clearly all romantic at heart, and started singing old romantic songs whilst crying and throwing flower garlands over Mozzy and Callum.

16 Paracetamols later, they finally arrived at filmistan studios. Everybody came outside the coach and proceeded to walk into the studio.

The security guards saw a whole variety of different individuals and said, "आप क्या चाहते ह "

"(What do you want?)"

They all started talking at once, like a gaggle of geese. All the uninterested guard heard was Salman Khan. He pointed northbound and told them all to go by foot as the coach was not allowed in. Ainsley tried to explain that he was a famous man and needed to meet with a particular director. The guard just made a hand gesture to walk northbound. He then mumbled some profanity and went back into his hut.

"क्या आप सलमान खान की तरह दिखते हैं? ऑडिशन आज। वेतन की अच्छी दरें।"

(Do you look like Salman Khan? Audition today.
Good rates of pay.)

Sonam could not believe her luck. She was finally going to meet him, up close and personal. She had been live streaming almost everything that had happened so far and her following had almost quadrupled, especially in India. She did not quite get a grasp on how famous she and her fellow travellers had become. When they arrived at Filmistan Studios and walked through the gates, it was almost a magical wonderland of actors, props, costumes, cameras, microphones, huge speakers and megaphones. Directors were guiding and shouting at the actors, the dancers were being choreographed to be in complete sync, and there were some extra spot boys standing in the corner. It was all quite extraordinary.

It was like seeing a movie in 3D while it was being made. In fact, it was all so surreal experiencing four Bollywood films at the same time. Sonam was in her element; it was like releasing her mind into reality.

A remake of an old and famous song *Tayib Ali, Pyaar ka Dushman Hi Hi* was being filmed. They all stood and watched the whole performance. The Transgenders were summoned to dance with the other dancers as extras, which they did with glee, overacting and panache.

On another set was a reconstruction of the song, *'Devil Yaar naa Miley The'*. Ladies in sarees ran over to the set dragging Anstey, Taylor and Callum. They all danced until their feet hurt. It was the first time Callum and Taylor had so much fun together and they could not stop laughing.

"Wow, it is totally amazing, divine and glitzy," said a very impressed Ansley Harlot. Uncle Joey even managed to get a beer from one of the crew members and did a little side to side dance, waving his arms around as though he was at a concert. In one of the studios, they had to do a whole shoot based on the festival of colours (Holi) which everyone enjoyed thoroughly.

Callum pointed at a handsome man with sunglasses on the back of his leather jacket, and shrieked at the top of his voice, "Is that Him?"

They all googled *'Salman Khan'* and replied with a yes. They ran towards the short yet sturdy man, who was completely petrified at the sight of an enormous, smiling black man and a large menacing looking white man joined by a big gang of transgenders running towards him screaming, "Bhaaiii", and two bald men 'Mozzy & Callum' who looked like they were about to have a bout of diarrhoea, and were just about to have a heart attack, so he ran as fast as he could. Uncle joey managed to catch him, and rugby tackled him to the ground and then sat on the poor chap,leaving him screaming in pain and agony. He chuckled and whispered into the man's ear, "don't even think about it!"

Sonam shouted at the top of her voice whilst pointing at the poor man, "What are you doing? That is the wrong guy!"

"Yes, you are right there he is," declared Mozzy, while pointing at another similar looking man.

The whole crowd of foreigners started to chase the other individual down, who ran into the crowd of over 50 Salman Khan doppelgangers. They teamed up and rounded them all up like cattle.

Callum shouted, "Can the real Solomon Kont come forward?" The plethora of Salman Khans all came forward simultaneously and declared themselves to be the real Salman Khan. Mozzy could not take it anymore and lashed out with all the pressure and stress he had endured, landing a powerful right hook on the nearest Salman Khan doppelganger, sparking him clean out. This led to a full-scale brawl, the old westerns, all the other actors, producers and the film crews started joining in the fight. Even the sound effect guys joined in with amazing sounds of how punches sound in Bollywood films every time someone was hit.

The trans women due to years and years of abuse and regular attacks from a very young and tender age were all black belts in karate; this was a natural progression, society rejected them so as a tool for self-protection they realised they needed to be able to protect themselves and each other. They started slugging it out and screaming in high pitched voices,

"Bachao, Bachao," (Save me, Save me) like they were the victims and someone was about to attack them.

However, in reality they appeared as though they were in a kung fu film and knocked out quite a few Salman khan look-alikes and anyone else who stood nearby. Uncle joey kept nodding his head in approval and respect every time he saw a knockout. He was quite impressed with the power the ladies had packed in a single punch. All the while, the music guys thought it would be more dramatic if they started playing intensive qawwali music from the great Nusrat Fateh Ali Khan at full volume. It looked and sounded epic. All of it was being live streamed around the world. Sonam managed to make a sharp exit in time and ran out of the studio grounds and into the nearest coffee shop.

The police arrived in minutes and arrested absolutely everyone. Anstey told them that it was a huge mistake and a misunderstanding and demanded to speak to a director

(whose name he could not remember) for his show. He was led away in handcuffs. All the major news channels picked up on this Bollywood brawl and it was televised all around the world. Even sky news televised it reaching all the homes in the UK, including Bradford. All of their pictures were as clear as day. Everybody knew them back home and if they didn't, they certainly did now, as now they were infamous as thugs could be.

Many B list celebrities from Bollywood started appearing on the news discussing events about the situation at Filmistan Studios. They all had opinions as though they were somehow linked to the controversies. Social media was ablaze as were all the newspapers. On the other side of the pond, all kinds of C list celebrities came out of the woodwork, giving their opinion on the crazy situation of people going abroad and behaving so badly. It was literally impossible to not have heard of the story of the English re-invading India to ask for permission to get married by the great Salman Khan.

Anstey Harlot kept on explaining to the ignorant yet very amused guards, that he was a celebrity and was quite famous, and there had been a huge mistake. What Anstey was unaware of was that this televised arrest had made him into a legend all over the world. He was being seen as someone who believed nothing could stop or block the path and beauty of one true, pure love. The fact that he had a lot of transgenders with him made him iconic within the LGBT community worldwide.

All the headlines read:
'TV CELEBRITY CHEF DROPS TOUR OF INDIA TO SUPPORT THE NOBILITY OF LOVE, STANDING SIDE

BY SIDE WITH INDIA'S FINEST LGBTQ COMMUNITY?'

Aunty Shaynaz like everyone else was watching sky news, "Yah Allah Ji, Taubah Taubah what have I done?" She muttered and slapped her forehead.

As they were led to the prison in handcuffs, an officer shouted down the dark and dingy corridor, in Hindi,

"बापू भाई को स्थानांतरित कर दिया गया है, उन सभी को वहां रख दें।"
("Bapu, bhai has been moved, put them all in there.")

The guard stood by the jail cell door and ushered them all in and shouted something in Hindi to the prisoner next door.

"वे सभी लंदन से हैं। वे फिल्मिस्तान स्टूडियो के अंदर हंगामा कर रहे थे और दावा कर रहे थे कि वे सलमान भाई से शादी करने की अनुमति मांगने आए हैं। इसलिए हम उन्हें भारतीय आतिथ्य दिखा रहे हैं। मैं इसे भारत का स्वाद कहता हूं।"

(They are all from London. They were making a commotion inside Filmistaan Studios and claimed they had come to ask

Salman bhai for permission to get a couple married. So, we are showing them Indian hospitality. I call it a taste of India.)

The guard gave them all a large metal mug each for (unbeknownst to them at that time) multiple uses, He then took off their handcuffs and slammed the iron gates shut.

In a heavy indian accent the guard said, "Have nice Dheyyy!"

"Anjoy tea, old bin"
They could not stop laughing and were very pleased and started patting each other on their backs, telling the guard what he thought was perfect English. By continuing to say "Wah Wah Dialogue" and referring to each other as London Boy, as they walked back to the office.
"SHAABASH!"
"EYY, LONDON BOYY"
"WAH WAH - DIALOGUE"

The Salman khan look-a-likes stayed in character and were posing and practising their dialogues, taking off their shirts and flexing their muscles, whilst standing extremely up close and personal to Uncle Joey, Callum and Mozzy. Quoting and acting like Salman Khan, in various poses shirts off and smouldering looks.

"आप जिस स्कूल में पढ़े हैं, मैं वहां का हेडमास्टर था।"

(The school you have studied at, I was the Headmaster there)

"Hum tum mein itne ched karenge ... ki confuse ho jaoge ki saans kahan se le ... aur paadein kahan se"

(I will make so many holes in you ... that you will be confused from where to breathe and from where to fart.)

"Bahut ghoor raha hai ... kya behen ki shaadi karayega muhjse?"
(You are staring a lot ... Do you want to wed your sister with me?)

"Ek baar joh maine commitment kar di ... uske baad toh main khud ki bhi nahi sunta."
(Once I commit to something ... after that I don't even listen to myself)

"Aam aadmi sota hua sher hai ... ungli mat kar ... jaag gaya toh cheer phaad dega."

(A common man is a sleeping lion ... don't disturb him ... because if he wakes up then he will destroy everything.)

Main tumhe shaadi karne ki pooree ijaajat deta hoon.
(I Give you full permission to get married.)

The unknown prisoner in the next cell shouted out,
"Main tumhe shaadi karne ki pooree ijaajat deta hoon."
(I Give you full permission to get married.)

"Main bhi tumhaari shaadi mein aaoonga, yah sunishchit karane ke lie ki ek vaada rakha jae!"
(Even I will come to your wedding, to make sure that a promise is kept!)

The transgenders were singing jovial wedding songs at the top of their voices to Anstey Harrlot and Taylor, while Taylor was busy staring at Anstey Harrlot in total awe. He kept telling the other prisoners that he was an enthusiastic foodie. They in return looked at each other in utter disbelief at what they had just heard and just to clarify they repeated the word foodie which meant something completely different in Punjabi and were laughing hysterically, whilst the transgenders continued dancing, clapping and being provocative around them in a circle. The songs did not stop as there was another one as soon as the current song finished. The ransgenders had so much energy. Anstey joined in and could not stop laughing while waving his hands in the air and joining in with the clapping and dancing.

Callum and Mozzy both sat in a heaped mess surrounded by a flurry of overacting Salman Khan lookalikes and started shouting racist profanities at each other until they just simply ran out of steam. They fell into two heaps on the cold concrete floor whimpering like children. How had their perfect world taken such a drastic turn? They used to have everything: the perfect marriage, their own businesses, the whole community in their hands and a beautiful home. Now they had nothing, whatsoever and were stuck in an Indian prison, doing jail time like convicts, with each other.

The other prisoners started chanting at the top of their voices: परदेशी (Foreigner), परदेशी (Foreigner), परदेशी (Foreigner), directly at Mozzy.

"हमारे देश से बाहर निकलो। आप जहां से हैं वहां वापस जाएं। वापस इंग्लैंड जाओ और हमें वह सब कुछ वापस दो जो तुमने हमसे चुराया है।"

(Get out of our country. Go back to where you are from. Go back to England and return everything you stole from us.)

A confused Callum asked him what they were shouting with such anger. Mozzy said, "They are calling us a foreigner and are telling us to go back to where we have come from and to return everything that the British have stolen from them."
"What A Cheek! Tell them we gave them the bloody trains," said Callum sarcastically to Mozzy.
Mozzy told him to just ignore them, as you always get a few morons in every community.
Callum looked down in shame, as he recognised his own past behaviour. A moment of truth hit him like a ton of bricks.

Taylor kept telling the transgenders that he was a foodie, which, of course, translated to vagina in Punjabi.

The transgenders were quite surprised at the way he was describing himself, yet accepted him anyway.
'This chap, even though he is brown, was born in England and I've told him and many others to go back home, yet here in his home country just because he was not born here, they are calling him a foreigner and are telling him to go back home?'
Callum for the first time in his life thought about someone of colour.

It then started to dawn on a not so ignorant anymore Callum, that England was the only place Mozzy had ever called home. Realisation of his home grown and self-taught ignorance started to kick in.

Marlina Korrot lived in Mumbai by herself. She was used, abused and broken. She was also known as the tart with a heart and now without her looks, after years of smoking, drinking and partying, she was a fat, frumpy and haggard lady who still tried to dress as though she was in her early 20's. Marlina saw the news, and was shocked to see her first true love, the only person who never hurt her.
She recognised him at first sight, Joey, her beautiful Joey.
She jumped into her jalopy of a car and drove straight to the police station. Mozzy's dad was in the mithai shop when he saw the news. Everyone in India was watching the drama unfold. He recognised his son immediately, even though he had not seen him for many years. His face was plastered all over the news and he recognised his name too, since he was the one who gave it to him. He really missed him, so he immediately called a taxi and went to the police station. Anstey Harrlot's Manager was absolutely furious and took the first flight out to India, armed with some of the best and most expensive lawyers India had to offer.

The transgender community in India were horrified at the terrible treatment their fellow sisters had received. They headed straight to the police station and held a huge protest outside to show solidarity and support. The high commissioner and the British embassy went to the police station. This had become international news and it had to be handled very delicately. Even the Punjabi farmers came in their tractors to the police station to protest so they could get worldwide coverage and highlight their noble cause. This was now a very big deal.

The British Ambassador was saying that this needs to be controlled quickly. He suggested releasing everyone immediately as a misunderstanding, which would cull the tense standoff.

The police chief said if they did, this would make them look foolish and every time an issue came up ahead, everyone would start to protest at every available opportunity. Due to elections coming soon and all the on line publicity worldwide that surrounded the whole situation in India. Ministers had to act fast.

A phone call came from the government officials, some say from the prime minister himself directly to the Sargent.

Fine everybody 500 Rs and release them straight away. Make sure you give a statement that nobody is above the law and

India is just in all its actions. *Jai Hind!*" These were the orders given from the top.

"My son," said a teary eyed replica of Mozzy, who looked much older, fatter and had a very heavy Indian accent.
"Come here, I am your father," He said when he stared at his sons confused face.
Mozzy's world came to a standstill, everything slowed down, went into slow motion and came to a grinding halt. Forty years of rejection, overthinking, torment, heartbreak, anxiety and humiliation came rising to the top of his head. Every negative emotion that Mozzy had endured since his dad left, came out in one go.
"Why did you throw me away? What did I do? Why was I not good enough? I've spent my whole life not knowing what was wrong with me apart from my skin colour!" Shouted a teary eyed Mozzy. Callum witnessed everything, in his mind, he wished he had the opportunity to meet his father and ask exactly what Mozzy was shouting out. Mozzy's father held him tightly and squeezed him, their bellies joined together in perfect harmony, they both could not stop weeping. Tears of joy and happiness fused with different levels of breath intake.

"Son, I have thought about you every single day, please come home. I will tell you everything."

"No, I won't go anywhere with you until you tell me everything!" Yelled Mozzy.

"I left the UK as I could not handle the racists anymore, we came to the UK to live a better life, not to be attacked and humiliated every day. 'Parki go home,' they would say. There would be smashed windows everywhere, petrol in the letterbox, spitting and being attacked by bottles when you are walking to the local shop." His father takes a shaky breathe.
Uncle Joey put his face down in utter shame as he knew what he had done in his past all those years ago as a juvenile delinquent and now he was witnessing the consequences for it.
"I could not take it anymore It was your stubborn mother, I begged her over and over again to come back to our home in India, where we would be accepted, but she kept saying she is British. She was so stubborn, so fixated on the fact that she was British and said she did not want to live in India as a second-class citizen. I sent money to your Uncle Walid every month for your upkeep. Did he not tell you? He in return sent me all your pictures and school reports." Mozzy's father pulled out his wallet and took out a picture of Mozzy when he had first opened his shop in Bradford.

Sonam had never seen her father in such an emotional state, so weak and vulnerable. He was crying hysterically as though

he was having an emotional breakdown. She came towards Mozzy and started crying. He hugged her tightly, this was her father.
Then they all joined together in a group hug and wept with happiness, joy and sadness, all in one go.

"Joey Joey " Screamed Marlina.
It's me, your Marlina. Look at me."
"What the hell?" Said a shocked Uncle Joey.
She went close to him, leaning her body onto his and put her hand over his mouth before he could express his profanity.
"Ssshhh, let me explain. He was dying, he was in his final stage of cancer. He had a stack of cash and took out a humongous loan. He asked me to help fulfil his dying wish. It was the biggest mistake of my life, my deepest regret. I was young, very, very selfish, stupid and naive. We blew the large stack of cash, then he passed away. I cremated him. I just didn't have the heart to come home to you because I knew you would reject me. I have always loved you and always will. I saw you on the news and am still in shock. I came here as fast as I could. I understand that you hate me and wish I was dead, I get that. But, all I ask is for you to forgive me for my stupidity, my selfishness and the fact that I not only hurt you, but I also broke my own heart and cannot live with myself anymore. I beg of you to please forgive me so I can live

without this deep heartfelt regret I have, like a grey cloud following me around everywhere. I have done so many terrible things in my life, but nothing will top what I did to you. Please, I beg of you. Come with me, let me hear everything you have to say. I will not stop now until you take me back.

Hours of pain melted in just a simple statement. The bitterness left his body like diarrhea after a dodgy curry. Everything he had dreamt of and manifested was now playing out in front of his eyes. All those hours of wishing death upon himself, on her, on all the ethnic minorities in the whole of Great Britain. All the drinking to dull the pain he had endured all this time was gone. Not only had it gone, it was like it had never happened. But Joey also felt light and young and full of energy again. He started thinking about his future for the first time in a very long time and it did not involve his racist patriots. Upon release, Anstey and his crew members went back to the studio to continue the filming for his India tour.

The Salman Khan doppelgangers hitched a ride with them as they still wanted to attend the audition.

The trans women got their manager to organise another bus for them to continue with their "Happy tour."

Uncle Joey went with Marlina to her flat in the slums of Mumbai to catch up on all they had missed.

Callum, Mozzy, Taylor and Sonam went to Mozzy's long-lost dad's home with him.

They were all welcomed into his house. It looked exactly like a huge, beautiful palace overlooking Mumbai's Juhu beach. It had a multitude of rooms. The intense heat was compensated by the beautiful sea breeze.

Callum again was humbled by the level of kindness and hospitality he had received.

Mozzy's father introduced Mozzy and Sonam to their respective stepmom, step grandmother and stepsister Amina, who was not married yet. She wore a headscarf, but it was a Union Jack which intrigued Callum as he could not work out why she would wear that flag as a headscarf.

Mozzy's Dad took Sonam and Mozzy by their hands and walked them up to a set of huge doors. He pushed the doors open and what they saw made them lose their voices, temporarily.

Inside the room was Mozzy's life over the last forty years.

Photograph after photograph, each with a birthday present underneath each year, just waiting for his son to return. His first day at Secondary school, a photograph of his first medal that he won at hockey match at school he day Mozzy got married, the day he had his first child, the day he passed his driving test and the day he bought his shop. He even saw the

loan agreement he took out from one of Uncle Walid's friends to purchase his shop. It turned out, Mozzy's dad sent the money for the loan he needed to open the shop.
Callum and Taylor were humbled by all of it. It was the kind of stuff you only dreamt, read about or saw in movies.
Sonam was overjoyed to see all about her dad before she was born. Her Grandad was a wealthy guy, who loved his only son more than life itself.

Mozzy wept and continued burping. All this time, all the hate and all the anger was washed away with the wave of tears that overwhelmed him. He now knew for sure that he was loved in the deepest of ways.
"But why did you not come for me?" Questioned Mozzy.
"Beta (my child), you had to come on your own free will," said Mozzy's father.
"All of this is yours." He gestured around the room. "Not only this, you have numerous investments and shares in a lot of businesses, hotels and property throughout India and Dubai." Said the proud dad.
Mozzy said he needed some air and left the mansion. Everything he knew until now was a big lie, he was an emotional wreck and was feeling very vulnerable, he had never before felt so emotionally drained.

Sonam and Taylor went to do some shopping, to get a bit of breathing space from all that had transpired.

Callum and Amina ended up staying home and told each other about, their lives growing up and as they started to bond realised that they felt some kind of deep connection. Callum kept farting; Amina never got bored of finding it hilarious.

Whilst Mozzy went for a long walk discovering the Juhu beach and rethinking his life, he saw and somehow built up the courage to speak to an English lady, who turned out to be an ex-British Army soldier.

They just glanced at each other and smiled t was Mozzy who surprisingly spoke first.

"Hi!" He said.

"Salam, Satsrikaal, Namaskar, Hello." She replied.

She had long, flowing ginger hair, the greenest of eyes, fair skin and the sweetest freckles resembling the stars in the night sky on her cheeks, and also had a nose ring.

"Let's go with the last one!" replied Mozzy.

They both started laughing simultaneously, it actually felt like they knew each other from a past life.

They talked and listened to each other intently about their past, their unforeseeable future and the pain they carried around all the time on their shoulders. They got teary eyed and snivelled whilst holding back tears, but then the strangest thing happened, they both burped out loud simultaneously and broke out into a fit of laughter.

After their laughing calmed down, they both drew close like magnets, bodies drawn to each other like they were the only ones on the beach, they sat together with their fingers interlocked. They then stared into each other's eyes, losing themselves as though they had fallen into a different realm.
Then suddenly, Mozzy's disastrous marriage problems overcame his every thought. Embarrassed and totally ashamed, he got up to leave, knowing the moment had been ruined. The beautiful stranger tightened her hold into his hand, keeping their fingers interlocked. She kept laughing a lot making Mozzy laugh even more in return, she pulled him nearer to her, but as they embraced, Mozzy noticed her left shoe was on backwards and he couldn't quite see her other foot.

Now Mozzy was not so religious, however, he knew she was a witch as soon as he saw a backwards foot which could only mean one thing, yes, that's right, he was about to make out with a real-life witch!

"Chudail! Chudail! Chudail! (Witch! Witch! Witch!)" Screamed Mozzy like a petrified teenage girl from a horror movie.

Without a second to lose, Mozzy got up and ran for his life.

He kept screaming, "Bachao! Bachao!" (Save me! Save me!)

As he ran, he glanced back and saw the woman chasing him.

 he was very close to him, almost outrunning him with a supernatural speed. He was so petrified, he did not look back again.

He started praying to ward off evil spirits, and ran until he completely ran out of breath, screaming,

"Chudail! Koi mujhe bachao!" (Witch! Someone, please save me) all the while.

Not able to go any further, he collapsed in utter exhaustion and then fainted.

The lady, being ex-army was very resourceful. She flagged down a rickshaw and got Mozzy into the rickshaw to take him straight to the hospital. The traffic in Mumbai was abysmal at any given time. This evening was no exception, and the rickshaw was stuck in a serious traffic jam.

Taylor and Sonam's hands were full of bags from their shopping spree. Sonam tried to hail a taxi but was unsuccessful. They kept walking and saw a rickshaw right next to them and saw a very distressed English looking lady holding a man who seemed to have passed out inside the rickshaw. Sonam had to do a double take and realised this unconscious man was her father.

She ran over to the rickshaw and said to the lady, "Hey that's my father, what happened? Who the hell are you?"

The sweet lady introduced herself as Bridget and explained everything to them.

"I think he just fainted." Sonam said and they all laughed nervously. Sonam and Taylor joined them in the rickshaw and told the driver to take them home.

They went back to Mozzy's father's mansion and managed to carry him into the house. Mozzy's father was quite flustered and asked his household staff to call a doctor immediately. The doctor checked Mozzy and said that he was fine, he had just fainted due to exhaustion and would be wide awake in no time.

They all surrounded Mozzy waiting for him to awaken.

A few minutes later, Mozzy gained consciousness. Everything was blurry and he felt groggy and weak. As soon as he saw the long flowing ginger hair, his eyes widened. He looked directly into her green eyes, before scanning her body. But

before he could see her feet, Sonam wrapped her arms around him.
"Dad!" She cried out "Are you ok?"
"Chudail!" Mozzy gasped into Sonam's ears.
"Huh? What do you mean?" She asked.
His body started shaking violently as though he was having a epileptic fit. "Chudail!" Screamed Mozzy and fainted again.

"I'm not sure but he keeps shouting out the word Witch." Replied Sonam.
"What does that even mean?" Asked a worried looking Bridget.

When Mozzy regained his senses, he explained about the beautiful moment that they had shared, talking and sharing their past and all of a sudden, he saw that her foot was backwards. They all, including Bridget looked towards her bare feet. They were perfectly normal. Mozzy explained how he saw that her shoe was facing the wrong way. Bridget laughed and pointed towards her belt with a pair of dangling shoes. "I love mother earth. So, every chance I get, I walk barefoot. You must have seen one of my shoes dangling from my belt as we sat down and mistook it for my foot being back to front." Explained Bridget.

Everyone started laughing. Callum found it hilarious and kneeled down, facing his trainers, backwards underneath his knees and shouted. "CHARLIE! CHARLIE!" 9while waving his arms in the air and trying to walk on his knees with his shoes on backwards.

Everyone burst out laughing.
Bridget decided that since they were all guests, visiting India, they should experience the Mumbai nightlife. After finally convincing everyone, they all got ready and headed off to the famous, *KITTY SU* nightclub.

On arrival there was a long queue, and all the gang got a bit hungry. Some street food sellers were selling freshly made 'भांग के स्वाद वाले पकोड़े' (Cannabis flavoured fritters).

The aroma indicated how delicious they would be, so the gang ate a bucket load of them.
It took them 30 minutes to finally get into the best nightclub in Mumbai, and 31 minutes for the cannabis to kick in.
An old song *'Mere Naseeb'* came on. Everyone liked the beat and started dancing.
They danced the night away, feeling like they were the main characters of a Bollywood movie. But, in reality, they stumbled and knocked into other revellers, spilt drinks,

stepped on other people's toes and offended almost everyone by projectile vomiting, farting and burping continuously.
Uncle Joey got into a shots drinking competition unbeknownst to him, a local mafia chieftain. He projectile vomited all over him. Luckily, due to the vodka shots, the Mafia chieftain had passed out. The chieftain fell to the ground, covered in vomit and was lying next to the bar, while his men were walking around, looking for him. As they approached Uncle Joey, he pointed towards the exit whilst standing in front of the still body. They all ran out to look for their boss.

After hours of terrible behavior, the huge burly bouncers frog marched them all out and took pictures of them and had them stuck on the wall of shame, so everyone in Mumbai knew they were permanently banned from this place.

They called three taxis and headed back to Mozzy's dad's mansion.
They all sat on the veranda, drank cool mango lassi and spent all night talking about everything they had been through in the past few days.

Bridget listened to Mozzy's life story in great detail and in that instant felt a close connection with him, she had found everything she was looking for in this poor, vulnerable man. He needed to be taken care of, he needed to find his way back to God and most of all, he needed to be accepted for who he is. In return, she could fulfil all she desired for her own sanity and redemption. Falling in love and a stable life was just a magical bonus.

They finally came down from the intoxication of the tasty pakoras and fell into a deep sleep.

Marlina and Uncle Joey came by the house. Marlina sat down with Callum and gave him a small cash box. She went on to explain everything that had happened to his father and the reason why he left the UK. She told him everything about the affair.

She said his only dying wish was for Callum to have this box and he knew that one day, Callum would come for it. He made it a part of the will that she gives him the box only when he comes to India.

Callum froze he looked like he was made out of stone.

"Are you okay Cal?" Asked Uncle Joey, sheepishly. Not getting a response, he knew Callum needed some time.

Marlina then hugged Callum and alongside Uncle Joey they both left.

Callum was just about to fly into a fit of rage and throw the cash box when Amina came next to him and held his hand and pretended to fart by making a raspberry noise. They both started laughing. Callum told her everything that had just taken place in reference to the deep conversation with Marlina.

Amina told him to open the cash box and then decide if he should be angry or not. They opened the box together. Inside the cashbox was Callum's first football medal. Callum released his pain. He held the medal, and he looked up at the ceiling and screamed out in pain, while sobbing and fell to his knees. Amina put her arms around him and sat on the floor with him. She waited until he calmed down and then encouraged him to keep looking into the box. Inside the box was an envelope with a key in it and a laminated plastic card.

It was a certificate that said,

Bank of Baroda

Mr. Callum Brown Esq. (Only)

There was also a small note, which was again laminated to stand the test of time, no doubt. It stated:
'Son, what took you so long? Not one day passed when I did not think of you. Well, I have left you a little something to make up for all this time.'
I LOVE YOU SON & I AM ALWAYS WITH YOU
LOTS OF LOVE,

YOUR DAD XX

The next day, Callum upon seeing Amina immediately was consumed with a new feeling of something he could not quite explain. He was however feeling as though he was not alone. Together, they met the locals and discovered the hustle and bustle of India. Callum witnessed poverty like he had never seen before, yet alongside the poverty was dignity, self-respect and kindness. He saw and experienced a plethora of foods, cultures and religions all side by side in harmony, with Mozzy's sister, Amina who volunteered to be his guide, along with helping him look for his son.

They got on so well. They made each other laugh and found it hilarious that she could speak better English than Callum. She nicknamed him 'Pudh'. She found it funny that Callum kept on breaking wind to order and beyond.

Callum plucked up his courage and said to Amina, "Why do you wear a Union Jack as a headscarf?"

She laughed and said, "My father bought it for me and told me that I had a brother and one day he would return to take me with him to England. He said that he would come with a gift that would make me want to leave here and go to England. I should learn to speak English and wear this scarf so he would know I am waiting for him to come back for me."

Callum's eyes were full of tears as he listened to her story and realised that had all they had endured not happened to them since that fateful Christmas eve. This specific meeting of the two souls' would have never happened. Callum for the first time in his life looked up at the sky and thanked his creator for all his fortunate misfortunes. He then released a fart that nobody would forget. Amina and Callum laughed and laughed. The rest of the household were not impressed as the lingering smell that revolted them.

That night Callum was awoken by a strange Indian disco music. To his astonishment, his bedroom had been transformed into a 1970's disco tech with lights and music to match the vibes.

From behind the see through curtains, Amina appeared wearing what looked like an Indian bride's outfit.

All of a sudden, she started dancing towards him and singing…

"Karloom Karloom Karloom Ahh jah Ahh jah Ahh jah.
Karloom Karloom Karloom Ahh jah Ahh jah Ahh jah."
The song was an old bollywood disco song which was called 'Jimmy Jimmy Jimmy Ajah Ajah Ajah,' however it was magically transformed to say Callum's name instead.

This hypnotic and magical dance lasted about 15 minutes. She then came closer to him. Callum closed his eyes and leaned forward. He felt her breath, then the delicate moistness of her tongue. He wanted to see and witness everything and opened his eyes only to wake up and see a huge gecko with large eyes resting on his chest, flicking its tongue out onto his lips.

His beautiful dream was destroyed by a lizard trying to snog him, which was now a living nightmare.

"Aaaaaghhhhhhhh!!!!" He screamed at the top of his voice.

But what he did next was very peculiar, he yelled out for Amina. She ran into his bedroom and immediately saw the gecko. She picked up a small broom and flicked the amphibian away. Callum was covered in sweat, breathing heavily. They both stared at each other for what seemed like an eternity, no awkward silences here, just pure love.

Callum let out an enormous fart which sealed the moment, they both ended up bursting into laughter.

Sonam and Taylor decided to go sightseeing around Mumbai. They became close and started telling each other about how their lives had panned out. Sonam confided in Taylor and told him the truth, the reason behind Aunty Shaynaz's plan.

She explained that the only reason they ended up in India was for both of their dads to get along and recognise that they were all the same and to give blessings to Samia and Hamzah and accept their marriage. However everyone knows how stubborn the two men are.

Taylor was sworn to secrecy and wanted to repay the trust that was shown to him, so he built up the courage and then told her that he thought he was gay. He justified it in his mind and confided in her as she had trusted him, and he wanted to share something important with her to show her that he trusted her and would not betray her.

Sonam was humbled by the extreme poverty and the disabled children who survived by begging. The whole experience changed her forever. She vowed to start raising awareness and to raise a lot of money for the cause of these poor children's plight.

Taylor met a pandit who explained all the problems in the world, accepting the fact that, unfortunately everybody is right. He told him many wise sayings and told him that it is imperative that he recognised that it was his life, and he was the author of his own book, so he should write the chapters as he felt fit and not to try and live to make others happy or not care about what anyone else thinks about him.

As the two awoken lions could not find their missing children, they refused to give up hope and with Mozzy's dad's permission decided to stay in India until they found their respective kids.

They would receive a text from Uncle Joey every few hours to let them know that he was busy looking for the missing kids, when in fact Uncle Joe and Malina were picking up exactly where they left off all those years ago.

Out of the blue no sooner had they agreed to stay on,

both Mozzy and Callum received the same text at the same time.

"YOU USELESS DOLLOP OF EXCREMENT! OUR CHILD HAS RETURNED HOME, SAFE AND WELL! HAVE A WASH AND THANK YOU FOR ONCE AGAIN, PUTTING IN ZERO EFFORT!
YOU ARE A FAT LOSER! AND YOU STINK!!"

They both read the text messages and did not react, as deep down, they knew that the degrading part of their lives was gone, and that chapter had ended.

Callum and Mozzy witnessed a lot of things together in India; it changed their views on life and they recognised and accepted that everyone deserved to be happy.

They saw bats at night, they saw the children playing cricket, they saw decorated elephants doing amazing tricks and allowing the public ride on them and saw different types of people religions and unusual cultures with their respective clothing dancing, singing and a togetherness they had not even seen in real life. Callum looked at Mozzy and said "Qubul" out of the blue. Mozzy understood and replied by repeating it back to him it meant, *'I accept'*. Mozzy meant that he will accept Callum as his brother if Callum marries his sister in return, and Callum meant that he accepts Mozzy as his brother. They both agreed to tell the kids that they will happily give their blessings for them to get married and it was not Salman Khan's call anymore. They saw the softness and kindness in each other, which was new for them. All the pain, anger and heartache had left the building. Like two long lost brothers after all the trauma drama and pain they had endured, they needed each other as one was the other's cure. They decided to visit the Taj Mahal and had to catch a taxi as Mozzy's dad said it was a treat from him.

Mozzy, his newly found sister Amina and Callum went, as Sonam was busy sightseeing with Taylor.

After receiving the text, they all decided to return to their beloved England. All of them had changed, due to their recent experiences. They had grown beyond recognition, became wiser and more tolerant. Mozzy's father and daughter agreed to go with them. Uncle Joey told them that he would be staying behind for an extra week as there were some things he had to do.

They called a taxi and within minutes a humble taxi driver, Mr. Karam Maliyh arrived. All of them climbed into the taxi, and started their journey to the airport. Callum looked at the driver and recognised him as the misfit who had first picked them up at the airport. The driver looked at Callum and winked.
The driver was up to his old ways as he had clearly not taken his medicines and morphed into many characters.

"Mere paas maa hai," (I have a mother) said the driver in an emotional appeal.

"Давайте пойдем к наркобаронам, возьмем все их наркотики и деньги, а затем убьем их всех, как они смеют не уважать нашу страну своими ядами."

(Let's go to the drug lords, take all their drugs and money and then kill them all. How dare they disrespect our country with their poison?)

Luckily, this time there was no accident. They reached the airport safely and waved goodbye to the driver, gave him a tip and hurriedly got out of the taxi.

-Chapter 7-

Good things happen to Good People.

"Poppi! (Jamal affectionately called Zesty this.) Hello! Can you hear me? Hello? Poppi?" Shouted Jamal on the phone. The reception on Zesty's phone was atrocious, yet he was very attached to it, as it was the last gift his beloved wife Sadyha had given to him. Jamal tried to get him to change it but he failed.

"Hello Jamal, my heart, my love, my favourite son, I can hear you very well. How are you my son? It's such a blessing to hear your voice, Allhumdullilah, I am so blessed." Replied Zesty Bhai whilst smiling.

"I am coming home to see you; I urgently need to talk to you. I have two very different yet important bits of news to share with you!" said Jamal with great excitement.

"I will make preparations to meet you at the airport, Inshallah. Please text me all your travel details. Mashallah, I need some good news." Replied Zesty.

The humble Imam did not mention anything about him being homeless and dishonoured. He told him nothing of how lonely he felt and how badly he needed him. He kept his pain to himself as it was his trademark. The reason why he did not mention anything was because he was worried his son would come to see him for all the wrong reasons. He did not want his son to see him in his current state.

"I am coming home in five days. I'm so excited to see you! I have to go now, pop. I love you. Take care, see you soon, Inshallah." Said Jamal and put his phone down.

Jamal looked into Talia's big, beautiful, brown eyes and realised that he was smitten by her. So, what if she was a Jewish? She was still a god-fearing lady, with a promising career as a heart surgeon. Poppi would be so happy.

"What? Why are you staring at me?" Asked Talia, smiling.

"Talia, Talia, Talia," replied Jamal, "I was in deep thought."

"Your Poppi will be happy, won't he?" Questioned Talia with a worried look on her face. Her dimples always seemed deeper when she looked upset.

"It does not feel like he is from this planet, he's an angel, I have never seen him be angry or rude to anyone. He loves God and he feels that it is a huge privilege to be chosen for his calling in life. I am so excited for you to meet him. I bet you will love him." Said Jamal with a humongous smile on his face.

"Absolutely. OMG! I will call him ABI-MORI, the traditional Jewish way to say Dad, I will have you know." Said Talia.

"I have made all the arrangements. It is so exciting." said Jamal. They knew there would be two marriage ceremonies, an Islamic one and a Jewish one.

"We will go to Tel-Aviv first and tell your 'eeh-mah', we will stay there for three days and then I will go to the UK to meet

Poppi and tell him. Then you and eee-mah will both come over to the UK. We will let them decide on ceremonies, venues, food, blah, blah, blah."
They both started laughing and then held each other tightly, the warm embrace made them feel as one. They were so in love and so happy; both with an amazing future in front of them. Whenever they held each other, they would forget to breathe. They often joked about how they would give the kiss of life to each other every time they forgot to breathe.
"I am going to miss you so much," whispered Talia.
"Ditto," replied Jamal.

Eeh-mah met Jamal and did everything in her power to dislike him and find faults in him. But all she found was an ambitious, handsome, considerate boy without a single bad bone in his body. He was full of love and positivity. He gave her the biggest hug she had ever received, which made her gasp for breath. He kept helping her in the kitchen and discussing recipes. He listened to her every word and agreed with everything she said. At first, she thought it was her Jewish natural instincts that were failing, as nobody could pull the wool over her eyes, so she introduced him to all her Jewish friends. They all loved him so much. He discussed all their ailments and asked their thoughts on old natural healing remedies. From a crowd of fifty, not a single lady of Jewish origin could fault him.

"He's a keeper," was the collective response.

Ee-mah with her friends even made a plot by placing a beautiful girl in front of him and left them alone whilst listening from the next room.

"I will not dishonour this house with your wicked ways. I suggest you pray and seek guidance and forgiveness. Please never speak with me again." Jamal said to the lady in his room. and then stormed out of the room.

Eeh-mah felt guilty, uneasy and queasy, so she decided to bake a cake for him to feel better about the whole situation Whenever he sat with her and she told him about her life, he would always hold her hand. The love, respect and light that emitted from his soul was that of purity from another century, from generations gone by, those who were honourable and noble. e could not wait to meet the man who adopted him and raised him in such a way that he became such a magnificent young man. She was so excited for her daughter to have met this man and from now onwards, totally trusted her decision making. How proud her dad (may God bless his soul) would have been today.

They threw an outdoor banquet for him the day before he left. He insisted on two weddings much to the delight of all the ladies. He begged Ee-mah to oversee all the arrangements, but said that he would be paying for everything.

Then the Dr. pulled out a little box with two diamond earrings in it and presented it to her. She shouted "Oi veyy" and started to weep in front of everyone. Jamal held Eeh Mah's hand and started to cry with her. Talia shook her head, raised an eyebrow and said, "Are you sure you are not Jewish?"

Jamal stood up and picked her up, knee high off the ground and swung her around. Everybody started clapping and singing an old Jewish folk song in Yiddish.

Zum gali gali gali zum gali gali
Zum gali gali gali zum gali gali
Hechalutz le'man avodah
Avodah le'man hechalutz
Avodah le'man hechalutz
Hechalutz le'man avodah
Hechalutz le'man hab'tulah
Hab'tulah le'man hechalutz
Hab'tulah le'man hechalutz
Hechalutz le'man hab'tulah

(From the dawn 'till setting sun
everyone finds work to be done.
From the dawn 'till night does come
there's a task for everyone.
Join together in a song,
Make the day's work seem half as long.
Join together in a song,
come and dance and join in the song.)

-Chapter 8-

Marriages
(Are made In Heaven)

After finishing his prayers and helping Mamica pick fresh herbs from her lovely garden, Zesty was enjoying a Romanian linden and a fruit-based cup of tea while listening to Mamica's stories from her time in Romania. This time it was about her aunty Ana-Maria, who taught her the secret of growing a good herb garden. Zesty bhai loved to listen to Mamica speaking in her native tongue as it helped him become more fluent and it made her happy.

It was at this most peaceful and tranquil point, Zesty bhai received the phone call.

It was from a lady, she sounded so young and well spoken. She referred to him as Poppi.

'How is this possible?' Thought Zesty bhai.

"My name is Talia" There was a moment of hesitation from the other side.

"Salam " said Imam Zesty bhai. "How can I help you, my child?" He asked softly.

It was silent apart from what sounded like someone just breathing.

"Please speak, I am here for you now." He tried to encourage Talia to talk to him.

Imam Zesty bhai, in all of his troubles and his tribulations, thought it must be a loved one of one of the prisoners he often

visited, so he made sure no matter what his set of circumstances were, he always made room for kindness.
"Don't worry, my child. Everything is a part of the lord's plan. Even if it seems hard at first." He said goading her to speak.
"You don't have to speak if you don't want to, I'm happy to just stay here in this moment with you." Said Zesty and she burst into a hysterical cry.
"My child, I am here now, don't stress so much. What is it my child, what is troubling you?"
At this point Zesty knew someone had passed, he started reciting a prayer, softly over the phone. As he continued reciting, the lady's hysterical cries turned into a whimper. She managed to somewhat compose herself. Then with a slight stutter said, "M-my name i-is Talia. I was studying with your son at university, and we graduated together. Your son, your kind, handsome, intelligent and selfless son, was on a plane last night, coming to meet you. I was supposed to be on the plane with him, we were so excited to meet you, to bring you the best news, the news was better than both of us becoming doctors. But he told me to spend another day with my dear mother as he knew how close I am with her and how much I had missed her whilst studying. He told me that he would go to see you first and spend some alone time with you, and ask for your permission, out of love and respect. My mother and I

were to take the next flight a few days later to come and meet you, Poppi."
The Imam was confused, she had referred to him as Poppi.
"You must be mistaken, my child, my son, his name is Jamal."
Tears welled up in her eyes yet she managed to go on.
"The plane that he was supposed to be on, went off the radar. They cannot locate it, they are saying that it's more than likely a crash, caught in a thunderstorm. They are trying to locate the black box. They have been searching nonstop. There is no sign of the plane anywhere, no survivors. All presumed dead. It's all over the news.
"Allah." Said the Imam.
He looked up at the sky and for the first time in his life, and shouted at the top of his voice. It was no ordinary shout, it was a man screaming in agony, it was a lifetime's worth of pain type of shout. It was loud like a lion roaring. The sound stopped halfway through him shouting, yet his mouth was still open as though there was still sound coming out. The phone slipped out of his hand and fell to the ground in what seemed like slow motion, and smashed into three pieces. He clutched his heart and took one last breath and muttered "Lahilah hah ilal lah hu, Muhammed ur rasul allah."

"Poppi? Poppi!" shouted Talia. Then the line went dead.

Zesty Bhai suddenly awoke, startled from what seemed like a deep sleep. He was confused as he looked around at his surroundings.

It was quite hot in Ttanda, Uganda. "Mfalme, wake up! You will miss your prayers." Zesty Bhai was shocked to hear a familiar voice.

He could smell his favourite food, Luwombo, Muchomo with Gonja..Katogo and Mandazi Sim Sim Cookies.

"Mmm, Malkia, I won't leave now. I will stay with you here, and I will not open my eyes." said Hakim.

"You silly man, you must get up. Come on, the guests will wake up now wanting breakfast." She threw a pillow over his face.

He sat up in bed and looked around. There she was, the love of his life, finally they were together again. He freshened up, his clothes were already ironed and laid out for him. He performed his prayers and walked through the house. It was not his home, yet it felt so strangely familiar. He knew where everything was, and it resembled exactly how he would have wanted his home to look. He continued walking until he entered a beautiful little garden. He saw that she was busy picking some fresh salad leaves and cherry tomatoes and putting them into an already overfilled basket. He saw a few chickens chasing a Cockerell, and three goats bleated as they walked past him It almost seemed like they were greeting him.

He rubbed his eyes and thought, 'Am I dreaming? Or am I dead? My lord, thank you for letting me come home.'

Sadhya turned around and sat on a soft patch of grass, rays of sunlight seemed to shine upon her, almost making her sparkle. She raised her arm and waved at him to invite him to sit next to her.

"It's ok, he is well. No harm has come to him, he will join you very soon. Olivia is very sad. Can you please help in making her smile every day until you come home. I will be waiting here for you, don't you worry." Said Sadhya in a soft and gentle tone.

"What? When I'm with you, I'm home." Said Zesty.

"Are you hungry? The guests are in the dining area, and you must greet them. They will be happy to see you." Said Sadhya.

Confused, he shook his head and said "I cannot leave your side now, let's go together." Replied Zesty.

"I cannot, I am not allowed. Go and greet them, they really want to meet you." Said Sadhya in her heavy African accent.

"Okay, I will greet them and then come back." Said Zesty. He stood up and stared straight into her eyes, while she gave him a radiant smile. He went up to her as she stood up and gave her a tight hug, lifted her off the ground and spun her around twice They both laughed like newlyweds, and then he turned and walked to the dining area.

"Put me down, you are a crazy man." Sadhya squeals.

As he sat down at the breakfast table, he looked around and saw that the guests were wearing surgical masks. He could hear shouting, and beeping noises. A massive bright light overshadowed him, the noise, the people, the light caused him to faint.

Imam zesty bhai woke up, and looked around. He was in bed in his pyjamas, and his whole room was filled with bouquets of flowers. He looked around his room, and remembered that he was in a little bed and breakfast. A beautiful young lady was holding his hand and praying. He tried to speak but was unable to, so he squeezed her hand.

"Poppi? Are you awake?" She asked and gently held a small glass of water to his lips. She had been putting Vaseline on them every day. After taking a sip of water, he started shaking and rasped, "Jamal!"

"He is here. He was found on a small island alongside some other passengers. He's just gone to the mosque to pray for you. He will return very soon."

The tears streamed down the frail looking man's cheeks.

"You have been in a coma for three months, Poppi. Your son has prayed from both your and his side, so you did not miss a single prayer, even though you have been in a coma."

Zesty's face changed, he smiled while the tears kept streaming down his face.

"Allah hu Akbar. Allah hu Akbar. Allah hu Akbar." Imam Zesty Bhai whispered to himself repeatedly. The hospitals were completely full, and they could not keep Zesty for more than four days, so it was decided to let him rest at the bed and breakfast. All of his expenses were paid by several religious organisations. Mamica had been caring for this man for three months and had asked Father Martin to come over every single day for tea and freshly baked cakes ever since she first came to England as she was a very religious lady.

The religious leaders from all the other religions, the chief of police, people that she only ever had heard of on the television, lots of Muslims and prison guards. Mamica could not believe it. She fainted straight after Patriarch Daniel of Romania, his excellency, called and thanked her personally for doing a huge service for Romania, and explaining how noble this man was. This man seemed so humble yet was clearly such an important man. How on earth he ended up in her bed and breakfast was a complete mystery. Whilst he was unconscious, many donations came in. A lot of people spent money on her humble bed and breakfast. She had been told by all the visitors and the phone calls she had received everyday, telling her about the multitude of kindness this man so selflessly had given throughout his life. She could not name a single religion or religious leader as well as worshippers of their chosen religions who had not come to see him. They came and kissed his feet and prayed for him. The entire property was engulfed in beautiful bouquets.Mamica had felt a strong attraction that she could not explain, with this unconscious man. She sat with him day after day and night after night. Her tiny hotel seemed to beam with light, and it was filled with a strange yet happy vibration. She told him all about Tata Florin and all the things they did together and how much she missed him each day. She prayed next to him and read the bible (in Latin of course). Father Martin prayed with her for this man, and he often wept whilst praying. Even the Pope facetimed and prayed for this strange man that lay in her humble hotel. A young Jewish girl moved into the bed and breakfast and looked after him too. She was often praying for this man; it turns out she and this man's son were doctors.

Many Muslim men and women came to see him and pray for him every day. There was a lot of food bought over, Eva and Amelia took instruction from the young Jewish doctor Talia, to send all the food to the local homeless shelter, otherwise it would end up getting wasted. Eva and Amelia started attending the Shelter on a regular basis and made a lot of new friends there, including their future husbands, who were also volunteers and kind, compassionate born-again Christians and they felt compelled to give something back, mainly the most precious commodity, *'Time'*.

-Chapter 9-

Happily, Ever After.

Mamica and Zesty got married with the full approval of absolutely everyone including Malkia and ran the B&B successfully, with an open heart, a warm smile and lots of kindness. Zesty reinstated and continued his amazing work at the Madrasa, bringing all the warmth and the whole community back together. The heavenly light shone through the madrasa again, bringing with it a full community brimming with happiness and lived happily ever after.

Uncle Joey convinced Marlina to come back to the UK and rekindled his love with her. They bought a small farm together in Norfolk and started producing their own chickpeas to supply to as many local shops and markets as possible. They smoked roll ups all day, every day until their hearts would be content; albeit their lungs took a bit of a beating and on weekends they set up a vegetarian BBQ stand at the local car boot sale for extra income to pay for their tobacco.

Callum Shakespeare became a devout Muslim due to the kindness and piety of Imam Zesty Bhai and married a Muslim lady who wore hijabs made of the Union Jack. He opened a new business where he supplied boilers and plumbing related stuff with Mozzy. Realising if they both fused their names, it would almost spell Moslem. They called it MozzLum Boilers

Ltd. and delivered their services to almost every Muslim household in the UK. They became happy and were cured of their ailments of farting and burping. They both used to attend every Man City home football match together.

Mozzy got remarried to a lovely patriotic English lady by the name of Bridget. She was an ex-army officer and had just returned from her tour of duty in Afghanistan. She was traumatised and just wanted to marry a normal Muslim man and try to make up for all she had seen and done in her stint in Afghanistan.

Samantha Shakespeare, (Sam) finally opened up her salon in Mayfair and had an exciting affair with a married wealthy Egyptian man called Arkhmed. He funded her project and loved his beautiful English rose Sam. He had a Rolls Royce, a convertible Bentley, three wives and travelled to different exotic countries. He also had a third home in Monaco.

Hamzah Shakespeare and Samia Shakespeare had the best relationship ever known to all in Bradford and yes, before you even think about it; including Rukhsana's and Karim's relationship. They had four children to keep them busy. Samia had a regular slot on the radio, where she helped the younger girls with their everyday life problems, preventing suicide and a lot of other different issues.

Taylor Shakespeare, the Chef, built up his courage with a lot of support from Sonam and eventually came out as gay and finally got a Michelin Star restaurant. All the footballers had dined there at least once and his dad couldn't care less if he was a poofter or that he was not a footballer, since he got to meet every single famous footballer. Even Uncle joey used to visit the restaurant and meet all the footballers. He did take Malina with him as he learned to trust her around wealthy, good looking men again.
Taylor became a world-famous chef with his own TV show which was filmed in Filmistan Studios Mumbai, India called:

> *"Don't Book it yaar,*
> *Just Cook it mera pyaar!"*

Maria Khan ended up in a mental asylum as she went money and power crazy and abandoned her daughters to move in with Christian. She started a successful accountancy firm and was wiped out by her lover who ran off to Brazil with his wife, leaving her broke and destitute. She completely lost the plot and only cared for revenge on all men, dancing instructors and Salsa.

Karma truly was a bitch.
The mental asylum put her on medications to calm her by sedating her on a regular, almost permanent basis. Mozzy was kind enough to pay for her treatment.

Uncle Raja Walid Khan (Zindabad) went to Pakistan to build his house on his land. The only problem was that Marpuf bhai was in debt to a big drug dealer and the drug dealer forcefully pawned his land and said that he would not release it until the debt was paid in Rutta. Unofficially, he was befriended and slowly groomed by the local drug lords who treated him like a real patriot of Pakistan, and they slowly got to know him well enough to realise how naive he was.

They were able to convince him to take a large box of Asian ladies clothing to the UK, which would contain a large quantity of Opiate drugs hidden inside. They did mention that they only asked him as he was a proper Pakistani. The clothes were for the chap's sister, Jaynah who had nothing in England, as her daughter was getting married. He was delighted and agreed immediately as he would do anything for Pakistan. He knew nothing whatsoever about the real intention of the parcel, especially about the concealed drugs; he was just excited that he was able to help his fellow Pakistani brothers. The drug lord's brother was serving a prison sentence, and he told them that the only way to release him was to give them a big drug bust, so Mr. Raja Walid Zindabad was sacrificed. The drug lord's brother was finally released and ended up shooting the drug lord as he no longer trusted him to call him an informant.

He was arrested at Heathrow airport, the solicitor said to plead guilty immediately as he had zero defence. He was sentenced to prison for even years (he resided at HMP Leeds). He could not explain in a logical manner, how he accumulated land in Pakistan for free and what he was doing in Pakistan if he was an Indian. If he did not plead guilty, he would have gotten 14 years.

Miraculously, he was finally accepted as a fully-fledged Pakistani gentleman in the prison and practised all his prayers. He also loved the fact that everything was free. The hot water, food, clothes, no bills, rent or mortgage. He got a job in the chaplaincy as a general dogsbody for the respective chaplains, on the request of Zesty bhai. He was actually happy. Given the circumstances, he made a lot of friends who spoke little, to no English and he was their representative. He started taking art classes and mainly drew pictures and paintings of his beloved land.

On his release, to his delight, he was deported to Pakistan, where he started selling his paintings and became quite successful as he was obsessed with Pakistan.

Aunty Shaynaz Khan, started her own orphanage, taking in children from around the world and became known as, *'Maa'* to everyone. Shaynaz set up her own radio station called *'SAAT'* which was run by women, for women. It was running smoothly and perfectly well, and was a real powerhouse for the women around the whole world. She was in her element and was grateful for all she had achieved. She also met a wonderful man who worked as a nurse in the children's ward called Mehboob, who made her tea in bed every morning and helped and supported her in all of her endeavors. He only lived to make her happy.
He was a Gujarati of Indian origin and proud of it too. He was an expert in Karate and loved a good conspiracy theory and often talked about the illuminati. His favourite drink was a latte, and he could not speak a single word of Marathi, although he did love chomping on a chapati, specially when he was at a party. The best part was they both wrote lovely Islamic books for children, she wrote, and he did all the graphics and made a huge fortune to fund the orphanages.

"Smile for the camera, everyone." Said the wedding photographer. They had a huge wedding in the grounds of Florins bed and breakfast. With so many brides, grooms, best men, maid of honours, priests of different religions, a huge flurry of guests, a great variety of food and wedding cake.

Ansley Harlott personally cooked the dishes from around the world, alongside Taylor. Fifty dancing transgenders led all the dancing and celebrations late into the night.

A huge toast was raised for all the newlyweds:

Mr. & Mrs. Sonam & Salman Khan	Hurrah!
Mr. & Mrs. Talia & Jamal	Hurrah!
Mr. & Mrs. Mamica & Zesty	Hurrah!
Mr. & Mrs Samia & Hamzah	Hurrah!
Mr & Mrs Callum/Khalid & Amina	Hurrah!
Mr. & Mrs. Mathew & Taylor	Hurrah!
Mr. & Mrs. Marlina & Uncle joey	Hurrah!
Mr. & Mrs. Shaynaz & Mehboob	Hurrah!
Mr. & Mrs. Amelia & Elliot	Hurrah!
Mr. & Mrs. Eva & Elijah	Hurrah!

Just then a helicopter flew over the wedding ceremony and landed at the furthest part of the bed and breakfast garden; an entourage, followed by a Bollywood superstar stepped out. Everybody went wild and started shouting and screaming after seeing him face to face for the first time in their lives. They whipped out their phones and started recording him. Within minutes all the national television channels appeared, trying to get a glimpse of him.

Amelia Maier married a pharmaceutical sales representative called Elliot who supplies pesticide to the farms, and she built a career as a pharmacist after graduating with a degree in Pharmacy.

Eva Maier, married a Mushroom supplier called Elijah straight after graduating in computer science and having a successful career in IT.

Anstey Harlot continued his magical; now all singing all dancing tour, and makes fantastic meals for the dancing transgenders whilst they sing wedding songs. The show has become a huge worldwide hit.

Sonam Khan, realised that all the facade of makeup, clothes, high heels and influencer girls online, as well as her side hustles, left her feeling empty and lonely albeit quite financially well off and decided to get married and settle down with Salman Khan (Oi! No, not the famous actor). Although, this particular Salman Khan was originally from India and was an honest hardworking local Muslim mithai maker who loved her dearly. She even enjoyed his silly accent, his sense of humour and him singing romantic songs in the mornings to wake her up. He made her laugh every single day. She was now eight and a half months pregnant and looking forward to being a mum. She made him mega successful through her social media skills and became a part time self-employed stylist. Oh well, a girls gotta eat right?

The Barista and his son looked at the lady wanting to hear more however, they knew the story had come to an end.

"There you have it, that was my tale. Now can I have another Mocha please?" Sonam smiled at the barista.

Sonam took out her bucket list and ticked off the remaining two items.

The Barista leapt into action, still deep in thought by what he had just heard. He looked at his son who was texting someone and wondered if he had even listened to any of the story. The barista did not charge Sonam and gave her a complimentary blueberry muffin as a treat since she was heavily pregnant, and he wanted to make her smile. He then kissed her hand and asked, "Was any one of the two men your father?"

Just then the two men walked back in with their respective families and started singing. Sonam laughed and joined in.

"Blue Moon,
You saw me standing alone.

Without a dream in my heart.
Without a love of my own.
Blue Moon,
You knew just what I was there for.
You heard me saying a prayer for.
Someone I could really care for.
Then suddenly they'll appear before me.
The only one my arms could ever hold.
I heard someone whisper "Please adore me,"
And when I looked, my moon had turned to gold.
Blue Moon,
Now I'm no longer alone.
I have a dream in my heart.
I have a love of my own."

They all joined the long procession of football fans and walked to the game. All of them sat together in the same row and had a fantastic time shouting at everyone and being animated as a newfound family. They all thoroughly enjoyed themselves. Shouting, cheering and even dissing the referee, in the midst of all the fun activities you would normally endure during a football match.

In fact, to be more precise it was a penalty in the favour of Manchester City. The crowd went completely silent, you could hear a halal hotdog drop.

Suddenly, Sonam let out a very loud excruciating scream and held her stomach.

"The baby! The baby is coming!" She yelled.

53,400 football fans watched the birth live and the rest of the football fans throughout the world watched it live on their television.

The commentators had a field day with all kinds of innuendos related to football, babies being born, and women in football.

"IT'S A BOYYYYY!" Yelled the commentator on his microphone.

No sooner than the baby was born, the baby let out the loudest burp in history into the now pointed microphones and the crowd went crazy. The noise could be heard from all over the north part of England. That day, a blue mist formed over the stadium and a star was born.

The crowds erupted and cheered, for once, it was the whole stadium of fans simultaneously.

The football commentators shouted "GOAL!!!!"

Manchester City FC said it was the first baby to have ever been born in the stadium during a match.

He, of course, got an immediate lifelong membership of free football matches by default.

The two best friends leapt in the air and belly gonged away, their humongous bellies bouncing of each other leaving ripples for all to see shouted,

ALLAH HU AKBAR!!!!!!!

The End!

Epilogue

The racism between the two gentlemen was the very thing that brought them together.
Salman Khan was found, and a marriage did indeed take place.
Everybody's dreams come true, albeit not all dreams are good.
Was it the wishes that were made under the shooting star on that fateful Christmas Eve? Or was it merely a unique collection of decisions made, leading to consequences that turned everybody's world upside down?

Acknowledgements

I have reserved this section for a huge shout out to all the strangers who have shown me compassion, kindness, dignity, inspiration and respect, when I was at the lowest point of my life. I had no idea what would become of me, yet these particular people altered the way I saw life and inspired me to be a better person in all aspects of my life without asking me for anything in return. What is quite interesting is that none of them knew me at all. They took me at face value and got to know me. They're the family that God gave me.

So a big shout out to:

1. Lulzim Murati: Thank you for opening my eyes, when I couldn't see.
2. Edmond Greza: Thank you for giving me dignity, when it was snatched away from me.
3. Chris Atkins: Thank you for showing me how to turn anything negative into a positive.
4. Sayyed Juied: Thank you for all the kindness of inclusion, and for making me feel like I always had a friend.
5. Abdullah Rahim (Dur Beta): Thank you for being my brother from another mother.
6. Rachel Hadcroft: Thank you for all the kindness and respect that you gave me.
7. Cenk Guclu: Thank you for always sharing, being kind, and tolerant despite your own problems.
8. Imran Ashraf: Thank you for introducing me to a 'No Excuses Attitude,' and your continuous support.
9. Berti Hilaj: Thank you for making me laugh, when I was supposed to cry.

10. Hamza Sam (Cool Noh): Thank you for sharing your insights about Black Power, teas, herbs and Islam.
11. Andy Pickin: Thank you for introducing me to the great Dr Arthur Findlay and Ether.
12. Patricia Anderson: Thank you for tirelessly caring and making a difference.
13. Mohammed Gafur (Cha-Cha): Thank you for lending me your shoulder, your salads, your hospitality and discussing innovating ideas with me, and teaching me how to become the perfect husband.
14. Joey McCarthy: Thank you for showing me a new path of manifestation and pointing me in the right direction when I was lost.
15. Ross (The Prince of Persia): Thank you for your hospitality, grand visions, your kindness and your beloved Camel hustles.
16. Naeema Gaibi: Thank you for all your support, blind jokes and sending all the love of Zimbabwe, Africa.
17. Dearest Zainab (Chatterbox) Chilwan : Thank you for your passionate belief in the project and for helping me get over the last hurdle. You are a truly amazing individual and a real inspiration, and you have no idea what a profound, powerful and positive impact you have had on me. I'm indebted to you and am forever grateful for your friendship.

An original and funny book, with many twists and turns.
A comedy based on the pursuit of fulfilling the illusion of true love and the role of a father. With a cacophonic start, the story unfolds.
Abandoned as children, life threw the two gentlemen many curve balls with nothing but disillusioned role models to guide them through the struggles of life. The two bigoted and hate filled local businessmen face the biggest shift of their lives with no control on the circumstances or the problems life will throw at them. Entwining football, marriages, racism, patriotism, businesses, homes, relationships, lives, religions, hopes, aspirations, cultures, countries and even pure romance. Will they both remain mortal enemies?
The bitter and twisted wives finally get to live the lives they have always wanted. What is the real power of a woman scorned? Women, when working together will not hesitate to show what power they yield, especially when they team up or their backs are against the wall. Love and truth will conquer everything.

Could a star-filled night really make a wish come true? An exciting and unique journey of discovery and reflection with hilarious antics.

Will the love of two young lovers cause a huge rift and destroy their respective families? Can you declare yourself a citizen of Pakistan just by obtaining land there? Is betrayal the only way to reach your heart's desire?

A Romanian family has settled in the UK for a better life and marriage could be on the cards. How one move can change the lives of all who encounter the meeting of minds, hearts and languages. The amazing dancing Black belt in Karate, the transgenders assist in the path to true love and happiness. Even Uncle Joey will forget about the diabolical mess he gets himself into and starts to eat brown bread again. The Imam trying to spread peace, tranquillity and kindness was always available to everyone, but what about them being there in his time of need?

Anstey Harrlot says you will go to the ball, while infusing aromatic spices. Will Imam Zesty bhai share his blue chilli sauce? Can the youth can change the world? And is Salman Khan the only man who can fix this?

Printed in Great Britain
by Amazon